NOW
I SEE

VERA JONES

A JOURNEY OF

PROPHECY, PAIN

outskirts
press

Dedication:

This book is lovingly dedicated to my mother, Mary K. Jones, who continues to guide me from heaven; my father William T. Jones, who at 91, still inspires me on earth; and to my awesome son, Andrew Soleyn, who since birth, has been my most significant purpose in this world.

TABLE OF CONTENTS

INTRODUCTION

March Madness for me, like most people, especially in the sports world, has always been about the excitement of teams trying to survive their most competitive basketball games to win championships. But for me in March of 2007, March Madness, survival, and winning began to take on a whole new meaning...

My mother, Mary K. Jones, was a bank manager by profession, but I told her she should have been a professor, because she had a PhD in lecturing me! She had a way of always giving me advice, often unsolicited, about what I should be doing with my life. She would say, "You know what I think you should do?" Usually, that rhetorical question would be followed up with, "Find yourself a good husband..."

In March of 2007, I was an assistant women's basketball coach at Indiana University. I was a divorced, single mom, so my mother and father came to stay with my son who was nine years old at the time, while we traveled to play in our conference tournament.

Sitting at the dinner table, Mom started in, "You know what I think you should do?" But it wasn't the usual lecture. She said, "You need to give up coaching. I know you've loved basketball since you were five years old, but you're missing your calling. You need to quit basketball; finish writing that book you were working on; get yourself on the speaker's circuit so you can inspire people; and then get yourself on Oprah! See, my mama *loved* herself some Oprah!

Our team went away to play in the tournament, and when I returned a few days later, my mom and dad headed back to Jacksonville, FL. Little did I know that was the last lecture I would ever receive from my mother. She died suddenly of a heart attack soon after. That was a hard foul that would take years to play through. I had never felt emptier, more sorrowful, or more lost in my life. It would take months before I would wake up and commit to actually listen to my mother. Without a true clue how, I wrote that book, and I got on the speaker's circuit. Just when I thought I was beginning to recover from the pain of my mother's sudden death, I then learned what a *flagrant* foul was all about…

One year after I had written and published *Play Through the Foul – Basketball Lessons for the Game of Life,* and subsequently began to gain sustainable ground as a motivational speaker, my 12-year-old son, Andrew, was diagnosed with a life-threatening brain tumor. Ironically, this also happened in March. The madness revealed itself in the unexpected and daunting pain of almost losing my only son. It was magnified in the seemingly endless trials of helping an innocent, unsuspecting young boy cope with blindness, bullying, self-esteem, and ongoing life-threatening medical conditions.

There were continuous wrestling matches with God, questioning why something terrible would happen to such a sweet young boy who had never even been in a fight. He had barely even gotten a taste of sports. How was I supposed to help him find the fight, the "winner's mentality" I often spoke of in my book or as a motivational speaker? Andrew wasn't a physically tough or athletic kid. He was a sweet, sensitive, kind, gentle-spirited, and humble boy. He never invited trouble. So why did trouble so rudely and painfully show up?

The fouls we both would have to unwillingly play through were not meant to break either of us. As a mother, they were designed to help me understand the hope, faith, and fortitude necessary to help coach my son through life's fouls. At the time, I did not realize I was also being groomed as an even better motivational speaker, author, thought leader, and seed planter. I was finding purpose in the pain, to help coach so many others through life's fouls as well.

In October of 2017, a video of a speech I had delivered a year earlier on stage at an Inbound conference – a Goalcast video I had no idea was even being produced - went viral. Tens of millions of viewers all over the globe, almost overnight, heard and were thanking me for sharing my story. Countless strangers suddenly became my sisters and brothers, my teammates, in the fight for a greater connection through empathy, and for healing against the flagrant fouls this life can occasion. I can still vividly remember breaking down and crying the night I first witnessed the video.

After only 3 hours of Goalcast's initial posting to Facebook, my speech had already garnered well over 500,000 views. Over the next few months, that number swelled to 43 million on that original thread, plus countless threads on various other Facebook and YouTube channels. It was that night that I came to the realization that a decade worth of pain was not at all in vain.

Just like in the game of basketball, we don't always know the outcome, especially when the fouls become so very challenging. But if you are going to win, you must first trust the vision that you can. I believe God put us all here on HIS team to serve, make the assists, help each other shoot our best shots, and rebound when we miss. And just like in basketball, the closer you get to the goal, the harder the foul…but that's why we must play through the foul…victory is often closer than we realize.

I never saw myself as much more than a basketball player, a sports broadcaster, or some poor kid's mother! Today, I know I am anointed to coach, inspire, and encourage. I now know that pain, perseverance, and purpose are three virtues absolutely necessary to experience life's true victories! This is a journey of faith and fortitude, from which my platform mantra of "Trust Your Vision – Play Through the Foul" springs forth. Sometimes, speaking your truth, no matter how painful, is the best way to help others live in theirs. I live to encourage everyone to understand that although in this life there will be some very tough and painful times, there are also winning testimonies for the tests, and there is purpose in the pain.

Sometimes, in order to really inspire, motivate, challenge, serve, or lead others, you just have to go through some tough stuff yourself. So this is my story. This is the story of my son, Andrew. This is our March Madness. And most importantly, this is my mother's prophecy! I'm trusting that the "get yourself on Oprah" part is still in the works! Ready, set, let's WIN!

Vera --------------------------------

PART ONE ~ THE LEGACY

CHAPTER ONE

THE PROPHETIC MADNESS OF MARCH

IT WAS MARCH of 2007 when my mother and father came to visit me in Bloomington, IN. I was a single mom, working as an assistant women's basketball coach at Indiana University. Our team had to travel to play in the Big Ten Tournament, so my parents came up from Jacksonville, Florida to look after my nine-year-old son, Andrew – we call him Drew. We were sitting at the dinner table when my mother looked up from her plate, and in her typical lecture style, she looked at me and inquired, "You know what I think you should do?"

I remember thinking, "Uh oh, here we go again. Mom is going to tell me to settle down and find myself a good husband who is self-sufficient and can take care of Drew and me, so I don't have to work so hard." She would say this with a melodic, matter-of-factly tone, as if it were so very simple; like all I had to do was run down to the nearest Walmart and grab one off the shelf in aisle four, next to the coffee. But it wasn't that lecture at all. It was something seemingly so abrupt and unexpected.

"You know what I think you should do? You need to give up this basketball stuff. Give up coaching, finish writing that book you were working on, get yourself on the speaker's circuit, and then you can get yourself on Oprah!" (You see, my mom *loved* herself some Oprah! No matter how rich, smart, or famous you were, if you hadn't made it on to Oprah's show, you couldn't be very important. *Purple Heart, President, or Pope – have you been on Oprah? No? Then who cares!*) Mom continued, "I know you love basketball. You've been in and around it since you were little. But you're missing your calling. You have a gift. You can talk to anybody, and Lord knows you've been running your mouth since I can remember. Finish writing that book, Cissy. Get on the speaker's circuit and inspire people. I'm going to write to Oprah myself! You need to be on there! You want me to write to Oprah?"

"Yeah, Mom, get me on Oprah." I laughed sarcastically as I shook my head. I got up and began to put away the dishes as Mom went rambling on about some guest she had just seen on the show. I couldn't help but think how bizarre and random her comment seemed to be. Basketball had been my entire life since I was five years old. It afforded me a scholarship to college, and then a graduate assistantship for a master's degree. It has allowed me to enjoy a long career as a women's basketball analyst for the NCAA and WNBA for various television networks like ESPN, FOX Sports, Madison Square Garden Network, NBA TV, and over a decade with the Big Ten Network. It led me to coaching basketball, traveling to places I couldn't even pronounce, like Prague. (I'm embarrassed to say, at first, I called it "Pray-goo," like Prego and Ragu had joined forces in the spaghetti sauce business!)

It just seemed so out of left field to hear my mother say "give up coaching basketball," but at the same time there was an eerie chill that went through me, as if my spirit was considering the grand possibility. "But what if? How cool would that be? I would love to get on Oprah!" Still, there were basketball games to be played. Along with physically washing the dinner dishes, I mentally washed the thought out of my head, and I began to focus on my coaching tasks at hand.

Mom seemed to have been studying me for a while and finally said the important, unforgettable words she would often tell my brother and me. "I just want to see you happy. Nothing matters more to me than seeing my children happy." Mom always had a magical way of just knowing what I was really feeling, a way of seeing through my best smiles and laughter, my hidden sadness, emptiness, or discontent. Deep down, I supposed I wasn't happy coaching basketball. I was content, but not joyful. There is a difference. Pure joy lives in the spirit of who you are, not on the surface of what you do. Mom knew that I was missing that pureness. Mom must have known a whole lot of things.

When we returned from the tournament, I drove my parents 15 hours back to Jacksonville, FL. It was a long but rewarding trip, as we had the chance to spend more valuable family time together. My mother, at age 75 and my dad at 79, needed frequent bathroom breaks, something my mother always made light of. She'd warn me, "Better not get old! You'll spend half your remaining life in the toilet!" My mother was full of whimsical sayings and laughter. I suppose I got a great deal of my wit and sense of humor from her. I come from a pretty funny family overall. Family reunions were full of cousins, aunts, and uncles, all competing for center stage to get the biggest and best laugh.

When Mom wasn't in the kitchen throwing down some of the best Southern cooked meals imaginable, she was sitting around laughing about favorite TV shows, funny commercials, and the good old days with her ten sisters and brothers. Mom's laugh could become quite loud and infectious. So, I spent a lot of time making her hee-hee it up every chance I could. She was by far the biggest fan of my silly antics and comedic riffs. I was encouraged to care about the happiness of others simply because she was my mother. What a blessing!

On one of the bathroom breaks along the trip, we stopped at a truck stop in Georgia. It was loaded with all sorts of souvenirs, gadgets, and crafts. If there was one thing my mother loved, even more than Oprah, it was shopping! Mary K. Jones, in a "find the greatest gifts, bargain-hunting" contest, was second to none! It was as though her most special anointing was to uncover high quality, valuable items at the best possible price. Do not confuse this with finding and buying something cheap. There is a huge difference, and she would certainly let you know how much so. In fact, she would sternly announce to anyone who would listen that "people ought to be ashamed of themselves for ripping folks off with that cheap mess," if quality was not a part of the selling-buying equation. Thus, let it be understood, if there were something of value to be found at a country truck stop, my mother would be the one to find it, or there was just nothing of real value to be found. Ironically, I think I developed a similar gift, but I seem to find unique value in people, who others may more easily cast away. More on that later.

Truck Stop Inspiration

What my mother found that day were two beautiful, inspirational wall scrolls; gifts hand-picked just for me. She did not reveal them to me until we arrived back at my parents' home in Jacksonville, about ten o'clock that night. She quietly came into the guest bedroom where I would spend only about six hours before I had to wake up to catch my 6:00 am flight. In a smiling, coy manner, she said, "I got you something."

I smiled and said, "Oh no, Mom, is that why you took so long at that truck stop? I knew you were up to something! Whatever on earth you could find at a truck stop is proof you have a shopping disease!"

She laughed and then revealed the scrolls. One was titled, "To My Daughter: A Few Words from the Heart." The second was titled, "Remember What Is Most Important."

I read each one with intense affection and appreciation. The words were so very thoughtful, insightful, loving, and impactful. It was as if my mother had personal conversations with the authors and told them exactly what to write. They are too special not to share:

To My Daughter: A Few Words from the Heart
~by Laurel Atherton[1]

*In your happiest and most exciting moments, my heart will celebrate
and smile beside you.
In your lowest lows, my love will be there to keep you warm, to give
you strength,
and to remind you that your sunshine is sure to come again.
In your gray days, I will help you search, one by one, for the colors of
the rainbow.
In your bright and shining hours, I will be smiling, too, right along
beside you.
In your life, I wish I could give you a very special gift:
When you look in the mirror in the days ahead, may you smile
a hundred times more than frowning at what you see.
Smile because you know that a loving, capable, sensible,
strong, precious person is reflected there.
And when you look at me, may you remember
how very much I love you
… and how much I'll always care.*

Remember What Is Most Important…
~by Vickie M. Worsham[2]

*It's not having everything go right; it's facing whatever goes wrong.
It's not being without fear; it's having the determination to go on in
spite of it.
It's not where you stand, but the direction you're going in.*

It's more than never having bad moments;
it's knowing you are always bigger than the moment.
It's believing you have already been given everything you need to
handle life.
It's not being able to rid the world of all its injustices;
it's being able to rise above them.
It's the belief in your heart that there will always be more good than bad
in the world.
Remember to live just this one day and not add tomorrow's troubles to
today's load.
Remember that every day ends and brings a new tomorrow full of exciting
new things.
Love what you do, do the best you can, and always remember how much
you are loved.

When I finished, I felt a lump in my throat and a heavy emotional tug on my heart, kind of like I experienced at the end of the *Shrek* movie when Princess Fiona reveals her true self as an ogre, and Shrek loved her anyway! Oh my! I'm having a moment even now. I digress… I was speechless. All I could do was try to laugh away the tears building up in my eyes as I gave my mother a huge hug. I said, "I love you, Mom! Thank you, these are beautiful!"

"I love you, too. Goodnight," she said softly, and she walked out of my room to turn in for the night.

The next morning, my pre-scheduled taxi picked me up about 4:00 a.m. and I headed off to the airport, with my new scrolls carefully packed in a pocket of my carry-on bag so they would not get bent or damaged. On the plane, I kept thinking about how my mother was always so thoughtful. All of her advice, the long phone calls we would share, with her regularly telling me what she thought I should do about this problem or that idea, and even her little gestures and gifts were all owing to her one guiding desire: "I just want to see my children happy."

Here Comes the Madness

Despite Mom's best desires and intentions for her children, I had no idea how unhappy I was about to become. About a week later, I spoke to my mother the day our team was about to play a game in the WNIT basketball tournament in South Dakota. I called her from my hotel that morning to check on her. She had been experiencing flu-like symptoms for the past couple of days. Her voice was very weak and somber. She told me she couldn't keep any food down. She felt weak and miserable. I told her to ask Daddy to go to the store to get her some Jell-O. Perhaps her stomach could tolerate that. She agreed that was a good idea and assured me she would. I told her if she continued to feel so bad, she should probably go to the emergency room. She told me okay, then she wished our team luck in our game. I told her I loved her, and I would call again to check on her the next morning...

It was March 22, 2007 and I was very tired and downtrodden that our team lost in the tournament that night to the Jackrabbits of South Dakota State University. We boarded our flight from a small airport in South Dakota, returning to Bloomington, IN. After we landed, we immediately boarded the team bus that was waiting at the charter airfield to return us to campus. It was about one o'clock in the morning on March 23rd when I settled into my charter bus seat, turned on my cellphone, and noticed the voicemail alert.

There was a lone, late night message from my father telling me to please call as soon as possible. He had left that message sometime just before 11:00 p.m. You know how you get one of those late-night calls and you just know without any doubt there is nothing but trouble waiting on the other end of that call? That was my immediate, ominous foreboding. My father never called me. Mom would always call, talk to me for an hour or more, then say, "Here, talk to your father." Then she would retrieve the phone after my three-minute conversation with Dad, and go on talking to me for another hour. With a call from Dad, and Mom having been sick for the past few days, I knew something had to be wrong. My worst fear was realized when Dad answered the phone to tell me my mother had died suddenly from a heart attack in the hospital emergency room.

"Noooooooooo!" I screamed at the top of my lungs in shock, scaring everyone on the bus. When I could finally stop gasping for air, I managed to mutter, "No! How? What happened, Dad?"

Adding more pain to the gigantic, gaping hole in my chest, I learned that my poor father had witnessed my mother's body go lifeless right in front of his eyes. He told me three ER attendants rushed in and placed her body on a gurney. They immediately attempted revitalizing her with a defibrillator to try to shock her heart back to life, but to no avail. Like that, Dad's wife of 53 years, my mother of 40, our matriarch, my best friend, God's angel, was called back home. It was just too soon. I wasn't ready. We weren't ready. Is anyone ever, really, ready?

There are a lot of things about suddenly losing someone so close to you, that just don't make sense. One of those things is this wayward feeling of needing to blame someone, even when there is really no one to blame. I knew that death was a natural part of life. Still, I blamed the ER attendants for not getting to Mom sooner to save her. I blamed my brother because my father said she was worried about him and he was the last thing she talked about before she passed. I blamed God because He could have, and should have, saved her. I blamed myself, because I wasn't there. "I told her to eat some Jell-O. How dumb was that?" I scolded myself. "Jell-O can't save you from a heart attack! Stupid! I should have been there! My poor father had tried to call me, but we were on a charter plane. I should have been there! My mom had a fatal heart attack while I was off coaching basketball, in a losing effort, at that! Didn't she tell me to give up coaching basketball? I should have been there!"

I was inconsolable with unreasonable guilt. I topped off the emotional blame game with blaming my mother for leaving me without warning! "You said you just wanted your children to be happy! Do I look happy, Mom? Do I? You didn't even say good-bye!" I found no comfort in the brutal silence that answered.

A couple of days later, in a tearful moment while planning her funeral, I reflected that maybe my mother had said goodbye after all. She had given me very specific instructions on what to do with my life that night at the dinner table. It was her last verbal discourse to me. She had also given me a couple of written ones - those beautiful, heartfelt scrolls. My mind began replaying how those words moved me the last night I saw her alive. Did my mother somehow sense it was her time to leave? I couldn't get this pressing question out of my mind. That final lecture and those scrolls were all I felt I had left of my mother's wisdom to hold onto. I placed my mother's picture on one of the scrolls and hung them both on my bedroom wall to look at her and to get my daily instructions, even though the words were merely lifeless repetition. I wished I could have more, but I was thankful that I at least had something sentimentally tangible by which to remember her.

On March 29, 2007, my mother was laid to rest in a cemetery in Palm Coast, FL. I knew my life would change dramatically, in more ways than I could imagine. It would have to begin with me packing up and moving from my home in Bloomington, IN. I had only purchased my home nine months earlier. It meant quitting my job and moving back to Florida to look after my father. It also meant being a single mother with a mortgage on a home in one state, rent to pay in another, and a nine-year-old son to clothe and feed, all with no income. Finally, it meant giving up basketball, just like Mom said. I had no idea how much she really meant it, nor that I would be forced into it in such a grievous way.

Many days, through a difficult transition, I put on my strong, secure, and lighthearted face to hide my inconsolably weak, lost, and heavyhearted spirit. I missed her laughter. I missed her love. I missed her lectures and advice. How I longed to see and to talk to her just one more time. I prayed incessantly that somehow God would break all of His divine rules, just for me, and mercifully grant me this one request. "Just one more time, God, please? Can You just let me see and talk to her? Can she see me now? Can she hear me now? Where is my best friend, God? Please let her come back. Just one more time, okay?" I'd cry for hours at a time, but to no avail. I had to accept she wasn't coming back.

Madness in Overtime

March of 2008 had rolled around, and I was preparing for another hectic few weeks of college basketball analysis with the Big Ten Network. It was hard to believe it had been a year already since my mother had passed away. I often wondered how I made it through that tough time. There were so many more challenges that kept coming. My mother's oldest sister, Delcie, lived 2500 miles away in Los Angeles, California. With no other family members close to my Aunt Delcie, I had to take a couple of flights over the past year out west to see her and look after her as much as I could. She had dementia and it had been gradually getting worse. At the age of almost 86, it had become apparent to all she would not be able to continue to care for herself, alone.

Aunt Delcie was a sweet-spirited woman who was very fortunate to have a couple of close friends who looked in on her pretty regularly in Los Angeles. However, my mother, who had been Aunt Delcie's beneficiary and closest kin, made it very clear to me that she expected me to be the one to look after Aunt Delcie in the event she could not.

March Madness of 2008 consisted of me flying from Jacksonville, FL to Los Angeles, CA, getting my aunt to doctor's appointments, and finally settling on the very difficult decision to have her come live with me and my son on the east coast. This was something my aunt adamantly resisted. In preparation to do this, I had to move yet again from the townhouse I first rented a year earlier, into a ranch-style home where my Aunt Delcie would not have to go up and down the stairs. The planning was so very stressful, particularly because it would upset my aunt so much anytime I even remotely mentioned anything about moving her from the home she had lived in for well over 50 years. Leaving the west coast to come east was absolutely out of the question for her.

Regularly in and out of conscious memory, the one thing Aunt Delcie did know was where her home was. She would always say, "Honey, I love you and my boy, Drew, but I don't want to live in Florida. I don't ever want to live anywhere else but right here in my home. I pray to God He just lets me die in my home." She would break into tears at the very thought of leaving. I would break into tears knowing I had to be the "bad guy" who would have to eventually make her. She did not have the money to afford in-home health care. I didn't have the heart to just stick her in a nursing home where I couldn't even come see her. Moving her across the country to move in with me was the best solution I could find.

Compounding the struggle of trying to reason with my aunt was my private, financial turmoil in 2008. I was living very modestly, trying to write my first book and figure out how to become a gainfully employed speaker and an author. My only income came from the December through March seasonal contractor pay I received from the Big Ten Network. The blessing was that I had a lot of credit cards. However, the curse was that I *used* a lot of credit cards. I went deep into debt trying to make ends meet.

At age 80, Dad was doing okay on his own, although he had run into a couple of medical complications. Andrew, now 10, was well-adjusted in school and could do a lot on his own. However, now I had to figure out how to care for a third family member, and neither my dad nor my son would be able to help me manage Aunt Delcie's care. Other relatives lived too far away or struggled with their own medical challenges.

When my mother told me it would be totally up to me to take care of my aunt, she was not exaggerating. I could feel waves of anxiety overtaking me daily, trying to save and juggle money to make ends meet. I still missed my mother so much. Her absence was magnified in the wake of realizing I had this huge elderly care puzzle to figure out on my own. How had I become the one who had to manage so much with so little, while still so terribly heartbroken? Forget how. I wanted to know, "Why, God, why?" But there was no time for "woe is me." I had a gigantic cross-country move to plan with a totally unwilling, unhealthy, elderly aunt.

In June of 2008, Andrew and I made the move from our townhouse to a 3-bedroom ranch home only two miles away from my father's house, which actually made it easier to get over to spend time with him.

In July, I purchased a plane ticket for September with the intentions of transitioning Aunt Delcie, at that time, to come live with us in Florida. However, God had other plans for her transition. In August, one month after her 87th birthday, He called her to her true, eternal home. God allowed Aunt Delcie to die in her own living room, on her own sofa, in her own earthly home, just as she had so often prayed and desired. I ended up changing the September ticket to plan Aunt Delcie's move to Florida, to an August ticket to plan her funeral.

I believe if you make it through life without ever having to plan a funeral, you are one of the luckiest people on the planet. Having to plan two funerals, for two close loved ones, in 16 months, for me, was tremendously overwhelming. I was thankful that my mother had done a great job of keeping her sister's important paperwork in order when she had flown out to spend time with her over the years, but Aunt Delcie had lost track of a few things in the year after my mother passed. By the grace of God and the help of a couple of dear, angelic friends, Joyce and Jan, everything miraculously got done.

With a ripping pain in my heart, one morning, I placed everything my aunt owned on her front lawn. I hosted an unofficial estate sale right on busy South Main Street in Los Angeles, where it received a lot of needed exposure from onlookers. What I couldn't sell, I hauled off to the Salvation Army. Somehow, a lot of things I never would have imagined could be accomplished got done in a short period of time: overcoming the initial shock and sadness; notifying friends and family; my flight to L.A.; meetings with the funeral home; filing and receiving the death certificate and other paperwork; trips to my aunt's financial institutions; notifying life insurance companies; the cleanup; the packing up; the viewing service; the funeral; the gigantic yard sale; the meeting with a real estate agent to put Aunt Delcie's home on the market; and finally my flight back home to Jacksonville, all in the midst of stress and mourning, all got done in a period of about 10 days. I had never before experienced that degree of mental and physical exhaustion. I spent many days, once I returned home, in awe of what had been accomplished under such duress. I had become a true witnessing believer of Philippians 4:13 – "I can do all things through Christ who strengthens me."

March of 2009 brought madness, but for the first time in two years, it was positive. I received notification that Aunt Delcie's home was finally going to sell. This was after the original agent I hired, tried to illegally scam his way into a $325,000 sale of a home I was only going to receive $150,000 for. The new agent, Pila, was very helpful in getting the home sold legally and swiftly. I was so grateful for her service. The call to say that she had found a buyer came at a time when I was $50,000 in credit card debt. I had just finished the manuscript for *Play Through the Foul,* that book Mom insisted upon her death that I write, and I had just pulled together a plan to start speaking and offering communication and team-building trainings.

With the $150,000 sale, I was able to pay off all my debt, finance my new motivational speaking and training business, Vera's VoiceWorks, LLC, self-publish my book, and have enough money to tuck away for a rainy day. I was just starting to achieve the experience and exposure I needed as both a speaker and an author to achieve success. The sun was just beginning to peek out from two years of dark clouds of mourning, thunderous confusion, struggle, and pain. I basked in the sunlight of hope, promise, and purpose for an entire year, until March 2010 rolled in.

For those who don't know, March weather in Jacksonville, Florida is very fickle. It's part of the madness. It's sunny and teasingly warm some days. It's windy, wear-a-jacket cool on others. March tricks you into a false sense of security with its sunny, budding flowers and trees, its cool beach air, and overall beautiful introduction to Spring. And then out of nowhere, the clouds move in. Big clouds. Eerie clouds. Thunder roars. Lightning sizzles. And then it rains. And when it rains, it pours…

CHAPTER 2

NEW BEST FRIEND

ON SATURDAY, MARCH 13, 2010, I was waiting at the terminal gate around noon in the Jacksonville International Airport. I was on my way to New York City to attend a Syracuse University Alumni party. I had just finished up my final broadcast for the basketball season and was ready to hit the dance floor to shake off all of the stress, not to mention the 10 extra pounds I had packed on indulging nonstop on airport food and arena popcorn for the past twelve weeks.

An update broadcasted over the loudspeaker and a squeaky, distorted voiced woman who sounded a lot like Charlie Brown's teacher (womp, womp, womp-womp, womp) announced my flight had a two-hour delay. I was getting antsy, as this was going to push my arrival time into LaGuardia Airport to close to 5:00pm. The party was supposed to start around 8pm, and I still had to catch a taxi to my hotel, shower get dressed, then taxi to the event. I was feeling pushed for time as I didn't want to miss any of the festivities! And how dare Delta Airlines deprive my fellow alum a single minute of privilege of watching my incomparably hot, old-school dance moves!

There was a bad thunderstorm in New York, making it difficult for planes to land there. After another hour of waiting, Charlie Brown's teacher bellowed again. Now the flight was delayed another hour! An hour later, a final announcement stated the flight was canceled. Canceled? I was frustrated. I had waited in the airport for almost three hours at this point. All of the passengers were asked to return to the gate agent for rescheduling or refunds. Dejected, I opted for the refund.

As I waited in the long line of the disgruntled passengers, I kept thinking, "Well, everything happens for a reason. Maybe I just wasn't supposed to go. I'd been traveling on the road for three straight months. Maybe what I really needed was to hibernate, not electric-slide and gyrate. I then considered how I had been away from my son, dad, and dog for a really long time, so maybe this was a blessing in disguise. I'd have extra time to just spend with them, now.

I drove straight to my father's house to pick up Drew and our dog, Dexter. Soon, I didn't feel so bad about not going to the party. I had to return to work at BTN in Chicago on the upcoming Thursday, so a chance to relax at home for a few extra days was definitely a good thing. The next morning, I chose not to go to church and just slept in. I needed it more than I realized. When you spend most of your time flying from city to city, hotel to hotel, your appreciation for your own home, bed, shower, and cooking your own food grows tremendously. I was quite content sitting in my living room watching TV rather than talking on it.

A little later in the afternoon, Andrew burst through the front door, crying hysterically! "Mom! Mom! Mom!" he shouted.

I leaped off the couch as he ran into my arms. "What's wrong, Drew? What' the matter?" I responded in complete confusion and despair.

"Mom, I was playing football with Noah and Nathan, and Noah threw the pass, and I went out to catch it, and then everything just went dark, and I flipped over the electrical box in their front yard!" he cried.

"Oh, my goodness, Drew are you hurt? Did you hurt your arm, your leg, what?" I asked with concern.

"No, Mom, it's not that, it's my eyes! Something is really wrong with my eyes! I couldn't see. Everything went black!" he shouted back.

"Your eyes? Well, can you see okay now?" I asked.

"Yes, I can see you now, but it's blurry. But I'm telling you, Mom, it went totally black, like I was blind. Everything was just dark for like a minute. I couldn't see anything!"

This alarmed me tremendously, although like the typical Superwoman mom, I pulled my son in close, hugged him, kissed his little head, and said, "OK, calm down, sweetie. You're okay. Everything is going to be okay. I'm going to get you into the doctor, okay? We'll find out what's going on. It's alright, baby." Andrew hugged me tight which made me feel like I might cry too. So much for the day of relaxing. It finally hit me why my flight was cancelled. My son needed me at home. I had no idea just how much.

Monday morning, first thing, I was on the phone with Andrew's pediatrician's office. I explained Andrew's blackout and urged that I had to fly out of town on Thursday morning, and we really needed an emergency visit before I left. The appointment setter said I could bring Andrew in right away to see Nurse Willa Price.

We headed over as soon as I got off the phone. When I arrived at the doctor's office, I began to tell Nurse Price, the Nurse Practitioner (who to us was always more like the doctor than the doctor himself) how Andrew had been experiencing bad head-aches and problems with his vision for quite some time, becoming steadily worse in the past month. He had been given two dif-ferent prescriptions for eyeglasses over the past year. I recounted the episode from the day before, specifically the blackout, which prompted the urgency for our visit.

"Hmm. This sounds a lot like migraines," Nurse Price diagnosed.

"No," I politely rebutted, "I know a lot of people with migraines, and Andrew doesn't ever complain of the nausea or light sensi-tivity. I don't think he has migraines. Plus, what about the total blackout of his vision yesterday?"

"Well, a lot of people get migraines so bad they get the blurred vision, and even blackout," she answered.

"Yeah, I hear you, Nurse Price, but I watch House and Gray's

Anatomy, so I don't think it's migraines," I shot back sarcastically. "Plus, Andrew has been stuck on 4'10" for a long time. It's like he's not growing, and we have good height in my family. What's that all about?"

She checked his medical chart. "You're right. Andrew's last physical says he was 4'10". That was a year ago. Hmm, let me go talk with the doctor a moment. This could be a pituitary issue."

When Nurse Price returned, she discussed an order for an MRI for Andrew. They had scheduled it for Wednesday at 8:00 a.m. I took Andrew to school and really didn't think too much more about things, adopting a calm, wait-and-see approach. I decided to return my focus to getting ready to go back to Chicago for studio work on Thursday. Except for the usual anxiety that came along with studio preparation, all felt normal. It was simply time to get back to work.

Poetry with Darth Vadar

Late Tuesday evening, I was sitting in bed with a ton of paperwork spread out in front of me. I encountered an experience I hadn't ever quite felt before. It was an ominous and eerie sensation, not really a voice, and yet undeniably I heard words spoken aloud. It was somewhat deep and resonant, like James Earl Jones as Darth Vadar had just entered my bedroom. "Write this down!" I heard. No, I felt it. No, I heard it! I definitely heard it; however, I felt it too! "Write this down! Write it now. Get these thoughts on paper," the spirit-voice said.

I looked over at the nightstand to assure myself an empty bottle of red wine wasn't present. No bottle to be found. I definitely had not been drinking. But at that moment, I thought maybe I should start! I was so freaked out. Instead, I chose to calm down and just do what the voice and my captive spirit were telling me to.

On my nightstand, there was a notepad, like the kind you get in a hotel. Okay, maybe it was from a hotel. Fine, it definitely was from a hotel. I stole it. Don't judge me. I reached over and grabbed the notepad, and I began to write with a passion and a muse I had never experienced at any time before in life! Out of mind and spirit came an amazing little poem, of near-perfect rhythmic meter and rhyming verse. Each sentence excited me more than the next. It was an uncontrollable and exhilarating creation bursting from my spirit into my fingertips. I could not stop writing, nor did I want to. Onto that little notepad, in about forty minutes, came what I deemed was a divinely inspired, spiritual masterpiece! I was literally out of breath, as if I had just composed an entire symphony, or labored through the finish line of a record-breaking marathon!

I slammed down my pen, re-read what I had just written, then I leaped out of bed, almost tripping over our Shih-tzu puppy, Dexter. I went flying into the living room where Drew was watching cartoons.

"Drew, listen to this! Listen to this!"

"What is it, Mom?" he answered back, startled and confused.

I could barely speak! I was so excited, I was shaking, and I felt like I wanted to cry – not a bad cry, but a happy one – like the kind of cry women get when their husbands actually remember it's Valentine's Day, and surprise them with a big, fat, glistening piece of superficiality called a diamond! The poem was my jewel, my priceless gem at that moment. It was far more priceless than a diamond! You would've thought I had just hit the lottery! "Listen to this!" I continued to my totally confused son. I began to tell him how out of nowhere this little poem just started pouring into and then out of me, and that in about 40 minutes, I had written an entire rhyming, poetic story. I had already given it a title: "New Best Friend."

Now Drew was excited – or frightened, I'm not sure which. He had never seen me so excited before. "OK, read it, Mom. Go ahead and read it!" he urged. So I began:

I used to have two very close friends; seems we were always hanging out.
One of my friends was named Worry. The other's name was Doubt.
We did everything together, growing closer over the years.
Worry would tell incredible stories, that sometimes would bring me to tears.
Doubt was a bit overprotective; she questioned my every need.
She told me things I shouldn't do or try for fear of where they may lead.
Those two truly looked out for me, and were always somewhere around;
Especially when I was hurt, and always when I was down.

As I read each line aloud, I stood even more in awe of myself. Drew was apparently in awe too, and he sat and listened without ever changing his glare, as I unfolded an entire poetic story. It was about a woman who was always hanging out with her two knuckleheaded friends named Worry and Doubt. The longer she hung out with these friends, the worse her life became. They would all go to the "Pity Parties" and listen to a band called "Misery." Until one day, her life became so dark and depressing, she passed out. When she woke up, she met a brand-new friend named "Faith." Once she began trusting and spending time with Faith, her entire world improved. The tagline to the poem was, "Stop hanging out with Worry and Doubt and make Faith your New Best Friend."

For the nearly eight to ten minutes it took me to read the poem aloud, Drew stared at me in amazement. I could sense his energetic approval. To remove any doubt, he echoed this sentiment with a roaring, "Mom! That is awesome! That is so good! You wrote that whole thing tonight?"

"Yes! Just now! It took me like 35, maybe 40 minutes! It's like I wasn't even writing it. I had heard this deep, Darth Vadar-esque spirit-voice telling me to write everything down. I didn't even use my laptop because it said to write it, not type it! Can you believe it? I'm thinking it might be a great inspiration for women struggling with worry, doubt, or depression. Oh my gosh, that's it! Isn't that awesome?" I tell you there was no modesty anywhere to be found in that living room, and I'd be lying to say I was looking for it. I *knew* this was the best of anything I had ever written, because I was confident it was divinely inspired. But why me? Why now? I didn't have time to think about an answer as Drew was already giving me next-step instructions.

"Mom, that is so inspirational! You have to make that into your next book! It could even be a children's book. It's not just a book for women. I think anybody would be inspired by that story. I loved the part about them all going to the pity parties together.

That was funny and clever. Mom, that is definitely your next book!"

Andrew was almost as excited as I was at that point. I hugged him and went back into my room; my heart and mind already racing with the possibilities. As a motivational speaker, I was constantly searching, scraping, digging for ways and opportunities to creatively inspire and motivate people, and here it was given to me without any real effort at all. "This is nothing but the hand of God. No way could I have done this alone," I reasoned over my new-found, divine and gratuitous, poetic gift. I revisited the "Why me? Why now?" questions several times in silence, with no true answer. Like all things, I figured time would reveal. It would be at least another couple of hours before I could calm down, finish studying, then turn in for the night. I had already decided on the title of my new book. It would be called *New Best Friend – A Little Book of Faith*. I slept peacefully that night, on top of a pillow of promise and purpose.

CHAPTER 3

FLAGRANT FOUL

On Wednesday morning, I woke Andrew up early, about 4:30 am, as we had to be over to the MRI imaging facility at 6:00am. Andrew had never had an MRI before, nor had I actually, so we both were a bit nervous about what to expect. We were pleased to be greeted by a personable and calming young woman who explained the procedure, then asked me to fill out the all-important paperwork.

Soon after, Andrew was escorted back for his MRI procedure. I went in the room with him trying to look at ease but feeling a bit anxious seeing his little body disappear into what looked like a large, white, pill-shaped time-capsule. Drew closed his eyes and told me he was just going to pretend he was on an important mission inside of a spaceship. That boy always did have an active imagination.

After 30 to 40 minutes of the imagining machine making a series of beeps and boops, grinding and knocking sounds, Andrew was pulled out of the time-capsule spaceship, and we drove straight for a breakfast snack, and then to Andrew's middle school.

Driving down the highway to my home, I was feeling quite scattered and behind on my research. I had a flight scheduled for Chicago O'Hare the next morning, so I was focused on packing and cramming whatever numbers and data I could. The moment I walked through the front door of my home, my cell phone rang. It was the doctor's office. The voice on the phone was telling me that I needed to come into the doctor's office as they wanted to talk to me about Andrew's MRI. I immediately told her I was really under a time crunch and was perfectly okay if they just gave me the information over the phone. Slowly and solemnly, the receptionist said, "No, ma'am, you really need to come in. We need to speak with you right away."

Silence. "Oh." I paused. "Oh, okay, I'll be there in about twenty minutes." I did an about face in my kitchen and headed straight for the front door I had only walked through two minutes earlier. My heart was heavy and beginning to beat so fast I thought it might explode. My mind went dark as one uneasy question after another began to form a line, crowding up my brain, pushing and shoving to get to the front, as each one impatiently waited for its answer. "What's wrong?" "What could it be?" "Did they get the MRI tests already?" "Why would they call me so fast?" "Is this normal?" "Why couldn't they tell me over the phone?" "Is Andrew okay?" "Oh my God, is it cancer?" Every answer to every question was the same. "This is not going to be good news and today is not going to be a good day!"

My car was racing North on Interstate 95, while my heart was racing South at record pace. The minute I arrived and announced my name to the receptionist, I was greeted by a nursing assistant who immediately escorted me back to a patient care room. Standing there, a typically serious-looking Willa Price, ARNP extended her arms to me and motioned me to sit down. Dr. Zoller was off in the distance sharing his gaze between Nurse Price and his computer monitor. Nervously, I took a seat. Then the nursing assistant shut the door.

"I think this is the hardest thing I've ever had to do," Nurse Price remarked with remorse. "The MRI came back immediately." And then she said the words I will never ever forget. "Andrew has a very large brain tumor. He is in an emergency situation. With the kind of tumor he has, it's not likely he will be able to get radiation to shrink it. I'm referring you to a pediatric neurosurgeon. He will further explain the diagnosis and your options for treating it, but most likely Andrew is going to need emergency surgery. It's a very large tumor. His life is in danger."

For the first time in my life, I understood what it meant to be frozen in shock. I could see Nurse Price. I could hear Nurse Price. But I could not get my mouth to say anything to Nurse Price. Time truly stood still, and I don't think I blinked for a solid minute, maybe two. I'm not certain I was even breathing. It wasn't until tears slowly welled up in my eyes that I realized I was still alive.

"I'm so very sorry. I know this is so hard. Is there anything I can do for you? Do you need a counselor to talk to or someone who can help you break the news to Andrew?" she continued.

Nurse Price seemed to be fighting back her own tears. She reached for me. I stood up and we embraced. That seemed like the best time to give my eager tears an opportunity to expose themselves. But I fought them off, as the Superwoman in me wasn't quite ready to be fully overtaken by this kryptonite news.

I released the embrace and I looked at Nurse Price and simply said, "No, Willa. I'm a woman of great faith. I will tell him. We will be okay." I said this. I actually said this. Out of all the things I could have said, I told her I didn't need any help because I was a woman of great faith? Since when? That wasn't my reality! I was President of Worrying Single Moms of the World and I had multiple advanced degrees in "Panicology!" Who on earth was I fooling?

"Are you sure?" I heard Nurse Price inquire. "You are taking this so well. Are you sure you're okay? Faith is great, but it's okay if you feel like you want to scream." She tried to comfort me by mustering a smile. I tried to smile back, but it was one of those ugly, half-smiles, like when your face is numb and swollen after a trip to the dentist for a root canal. I then spoke slowly, "I'm sure at some point I will."

Some point came fast. As soon as I made it out to the parking lot and sat down in my car, out came a howling roar of a wounded lion. I screamed, "Nooooo! Not my baby! Not my Drewbear! No, God, no! Why? Why? You took my mother and now You want to take my only child? Why God? Whyyyyy?" I cried so hard I felt like I was going to throw up. I opened the car door and just leaned up against it, sobbing uncontrollably and gasping for air. I felt like I might faint. I lost track of time and tears, until the most sobering thought hit me. I realized that I still had to somehow break this news to my beloved Drew. How on earth do you tell a sweet and innocent 12-year-old boy that his life is in danger because of a brain tumor? He didn't deserve this! I didn't deserve this either! How was I supposed to get him through this? I screamed, "God, please help me! Please! I can't take any more! I'm not strong enough!"

When I finally found the strength to get back in the car (Lord only knows where it came from), I called Andrew's father, Stephen. I was still crying hysterically but trying my best to gather myself. The moment he answered the phone, I was crying so hard he could not hear me. Impatient, frightened, and annoyed, he yelled at me to calm down. I was trying to. It was like an anvil was placed on my tongue and it took every piece of my soul to move it out of the way just enough to speak clearly.

When I was able to settle just enough to mumble "Andrew has a brain tumor," I sensed the shock had taken over Stephen too. I could hear him choking up, saying, "Oh no. God, no!" Through my sobbing, I heard him ask how I was going to break it to Andrew. I didn't have that answered yet. I was barely breaking it to myself! The more we talked, the worse I felt. I was beginning to feel anger that Stephen was yelling at me to be calmer. I wanted to yell back, "Easy for you to say! You're not here!" but the anvil got heavier in my mouth and I sensed I might choke. Stephen lived 1,000 miles away in New York. We had been separated and divorced a decade and I never cared much about the geographical distance between us. But I was officially experiencing the heat of my hell on earth at that moment, and

I was furious that Stephen wasn't around when Andrew and I both needed him more than ever.

The tongue anvil lifted. "Stop yelling at me to calm down!" I lashed out!

Stephen tried to explain, "No, I'm just trying to help you stay calm. You're screaming, and I can barely understand you, and you're going to make yourself…"

My mind was raging with pain, blame, anger, sorrow, helplessness, fear, and worry all at the same time! I knew yelling at Stephen was wrong, hurtful, and pointless, but no part of me regained the sensibility to be reasonable or logical. So, I just hung up the phone totally indifferent to how Stephen must have been feeling and truly perplexed how the air I once breathed so freely could suddenly be so very void of oxygen. I was confident I was about to pass out.

Darth Vadar Returns

Everything was a complete blur, but somehow, I ended up behind the wheel of my car, driving frantically down the highway, trying to get home. I gripped the steering wheel tightly and flipped on the windshield wipers, not realizing the watery glare obstructing my view wasn't from rain, but from my own tumultuous tears. I was rocking back and forth, crying and mumbling, "God, please help me. Save him. I don't know what to do. Help me. This hurts so bad. I'm so scared. Please, God, I don't know what to dooo!" Then I abruptly became silent. I slapped the steering wheel hard and gripped it tighter and began to mutter over and over again the very words I had just written the night before. It was the tag-line to the poem about Faith.

"Stop hanging out with Worry and Doubt and make FAITH your New Best Friend." I said it again, "Stop hanging out with Worry and Doubt and make FAITH your New Best Friend." A little louder, I said it again, "Stop hanging out with Worry and Doubt and make FAITH your New Best Friend!" Again! Again! Again! I began screaming it the entire way home, realizing that divine spirit was covering me, and had been covering me since the night before when I thought Darth Vadar was in my bedroom. The poem about Faith was the Holy Spirit preparing me for spiritual warfare. It wasn't about what I could do. It was about my faith that God had already taken care of Andrew. My Drew was already healed, but I had to be of good courage to see it all come to pass. No matter what it felt like, no matter what it looked like, no matter what anyone else said, I had been given an instruction on how to get Drew and myself through this:

"Stop hanging out with Worry and Doubt and make FAITH your New Best Friend!"

That thought, that meditational mantra, carried me home. I waited on the sofa for Andrew to come home from school. When he walked in the door, I inhaled so hard I practically rearranged the living room furniture. I asked Drew how school was. The typical "fine," he answered. I asked him to come sit down with me on the sofa.

"Drew, remember that poem that seemed to miraculously come out of me last night?" I asked.

"Yeah, the one about Faith? Did you call a publisher? You're going to make it into a book?" Andrew inquired.

"No, sweetie, not yet. I went back to your doctor today. Um, you see, I don't think that story popped into my spirit last night for everyone else just yet. I think God intended that story about Faith for you and me. Drew, Nurse Price says the reason you've been having all those headaches and what happened when you were playing football was because you have a brain tumor." I was trying to keep a straight face, fighting back a well of tears. I knew it was important for me to be strong because Drew always played off of my emotions. I continued on, "So you will have to have surgery right away to have the tumor removed." I waited to see how he would respond. He didn't. The silence and the innocent confusion and hurt on his face said it all.

"Are you okay, sweetie? I know this is hard, but I also know there is no way in the world God would give us our own story about faith the night before we found this out. He wants us to be strong and trust that everything is going to work out just fine. Okay, baby? It's you and me who have to stop hanging out with Worry and Doubt and make Faith our New Best Friend, Okay?"

"Okay," Andrew answered more out of obedience than belief, I could tell. I hugged him for as long as he would stay connected to me. When he released, he went to his bedroom, while I went to mine. I'm pretty certain we both had a good cry, and asked God a lot of questions of "Why?" It all seemed so very unfair. I know most mothers think their children are innocent little angels. But mine really was. He had a huge, loving heart. His teachers wanted to clone his good spirit and love for learning. Everyone that ever met him adored him, except for a few bully-types at school. At twelve years old, the boy had never even had a fight with anyone. He was a quiet, sweet, straight-A, gifted, smiling, nerdy type. He took pride in his nerdiness, once announcing to me when he was seven years old, "Mom, I don't care if I'm a nerd. If God made me this way, then I'm okay with it."

Why would God allow this to happen to someone who has never hurt anyone? He was already born hearing impaired, a diagnosis that didn't show up until he was three and a half years old. When I asked how it was that the boy was already three years old and I was just finding out he was hearing impaired, the audiologist suggested maybe I talked so loud Andrew never missed a beat! Well, I didn't know much, but I knew I needed to find a new audiologist! But maybe there was some truth to his facetiousness. Drew had always responded according to my voice, my lead. He was always supersensitive, tremendously in tune with my emotions. How could I talk to him about faith and courage and strength if mine was waning? I had to be strong and faithful first, setting the tone and mindset for my poor son. It was a tremendously heavy assignment. So in my bedroom, struggling to breathe, I had to check with God for a lot of unanswered questions.

"God, I love that boy so much! He's my whole world. Why are You doing this to him? To me? What have we done? First, Mom, then Aunt Delcie, and now my Drew? Why? It's just too much. I can't do this!" I had gone from a strong Supermom finding the right words to tell her only son he had a brain tumor, to a weak struggle-mom who could not find enough words from God to stop herself from crying. The devil found my kryptonite. All of the strength, courage, wisdom, and faith I thought I had built up after I wrote my first book, *Play Through the Foul*, after Mom died, seemed to totally disappear. This wasn't an ordinary foul. This wasn't a "slap on the wrist by the opponent while trying to shoot the ball" kind of foul. This was the opponent's entire team gang-tackling me to the ground then beating me near-death! Flagrant Foul, Ref! Flagrant!

Depressing Diagnoses and Decisions

With this thought came a far more important one. What on earth is Drew feeling? Forget about what I feel. What is my 12-year-old, smiling, biscuit-loving son going through? I shouted at myself in shame, "Pull yourself together, Vera! That boy needs you! You have to be strong! You HAVE to!" I learned right then that sometimes being strong is not an option; it is the only choice you have.

Within 6 hours of hearing about Andrew's fate, my best friend, Jan, who lived 5.5 hours away had already packed a suitcase, gassed up her car, and was at the front door of our home. Jan had always shared a special bond with Drew. They called each other soulmates because they shared the same birthday. Jan's face was the first one I saw in a tumultuous day other than the faces of the doctors, nurses and, of course, Drew's. It was the face of an angel at that moment. Never before did I fully understand the meaning of "We all need each other." To this day, I'm not sure what I would have done had she not arrived.

It was Jan that went with Drew and me to Dr. Ian Heger's office. He was the pediatric neurosurgeon who spoke unto me the most haunting and daunting words I had ever heard. When we arrived at Wolfson's Children's Hospital in Jacksonville, FL, Dr. Heger presented the image of Andrew's brain on a large screen indicating exactly where the tumor was located. He explained that it was his surgical team's belief that the kind of tumor Andrew had was a "craniopharyngioma." Andrew, who had a very significant interest in science, looked on with seemingly more curiosity than concern. Soon after asking Andrew if he had any questions, Jan took Drew out to another room so that Dr. Heger could speak with me directly, alone.

"Andrew is in a very difficult predicament. A craniopharyngioma is a relatively rare tumor, but it does occur most often in children, usually between the ages of five and eleven." He referenced the enlarged image of Drew's brain. "The tumor is sitting on what we call the optic chiasm. It is pressing on his optic nerve, but it is also significantly hovering here, over his pituitary gland which controls hormonal function. Typically, when we encounter brain tumors in general, there is an option to possibly try to shrink it with radiation. However, because of the size and the placement of Andrew's tumor, it is my best recommendation we do not wait and see. I recommend we proceed with emergency surgery to extract as much of the tumor as we can. I believe I can get all of it."

Dr. Heger took a breath. I don't think I did. I was a zombie at attention. He continued, "Craniopharyngiomas are not known to be cancerous, but there is also no way to be 100-percent sure what kind of tumor it is if we don't get in there and perform a biopsy. What I am saying, however, is that if I'm going to go in there at all, I truly believe it's best to just go in and get that thing out of there, regardless. The decision of how we proceed, of course, is up to you. Without the surgery, Andrew does not have a very favorable prognosis. You must also know, there are reasonable complications associated with performing the surgery that I must disclose to you so you can make the best, informed decision."

I stared at Dr. Ian Heger more focused and intently than I've ever stared at any rich, good- looking man in my life. I'm almost certain I didn't blink, and I don't remember exhaling until he was through. The only thing I remember was having an odd thought about being thankful for tough skin that was holding all of my insides in place, as I could feel every organ threatening to explode and ooze out all over that pristine clean pediatric neurosurgery office. Dr. Heger continued, pulling no punches. Every sentence was either a jab that went straight to my gut or an uppercut to my chin.

"There's a good chance that your son may die; but, we are going to do everything we can to save him. Even if Andrew lives, there is a good chance he will be blind; but, I'm going to do everything in my power to protect his sight. In the event that Andrew lives, you both are in for a very long road. Because of how much the tumor has already damaged his pituitary gland, it is very likely that the removal of the tumor will cause significantly more damage. He may lose all pituitary function. What this means is that all of the hormones that this gland makes daily to keep us alive, such as testosterone, cortisol, growth hormones, etc. will all have to be artificially manufactured and administered for Andrew."

Dr. Heger then began to rattle off a list of the most unimaginable ailments, issues, concerns, and problems, all with a life-threatening caveat:

"Andrew will likely feel insatiable. No matter how much he eats, he will always feel hungry. Without pituitary and hypothalamus function, he won't have the ability to know when he is full. This, of course, will put him at high risk for obesity issues. He may experience serious problems with diabetes, heart disease, and possible liver ailments. He will have to be under constant watch and care. He will need the support of a nutritionist. I've known parents who have had to go so far as to put a lock on the refrigerator and pantry. It can become that psychologically intense.

Andrew will likely have diabetes insipidus, often called water diabetes, which is a disorder where he will have periods of extreme dehydration, excessive thirst, and frequent urination. Andrew will have to urinate sometimes as much as five times the amount of the average person. He may take in gallons of water and still never feel his thirst is satiated. Without his pituitary function, his kidneys do not know when it is time to stop urinating. So, like a water hose, he will just keep peeing, while constantly having extreme thirst as his body is trying to drink back what his kidneys pee out. It is impossible to do this fast enough, so people with this condition run the risk of death due to extreme dehydration. This could happen in a matter of just a couple of hours. Therefore, we have to regulate this crucial bodily function through medication. A missed dosage may require a 911 call for an IV of fluids and meds to give an endocrinologist time to evaluate him and get his water balance back on track."

In addition to trying to understand Drew's dramatic prognosis for blindness, I was struggling to process Dr. Heger's words I'd never heard before, couldn't spell, or adequately pronounce. I kept thinking blaming thoughts like, "Why didn't I pay more attention in biology class? Pituitary gland? Sheesh, I remember something about that, but I just can't recall it being so very serious. Cranio-what? Endo-what? Hypo-what? What did you say about him peeing all the time? Wait! When do I call 911? What did you say about diabetes? His liver? Didn't you also say something about his kidneys? Dang it all!!" Just when I prayed Dr. Heger was done, he went on with the medical science lecture some more! This blow felt like the final knockout punch.

"I should also advise you about adrenal insufficiency. Without pituitary function, Andrew will not have the ability to make adrenaline. When you or I get injured, say a broken leg, adrenaline rushes through our body and this hormonal agent protects us from going into shock from the pain or damage caused by the injury. It actually saves our lives. The same goes for when we get sick and our body goes into a fever. Adrenaline helps us manage that intense change to our system. Andrew would not have this self-protection. He would have to have it injected into his system immediately, say within 15 minutes of injury or fever over 101 degrees. Without it, he would die. So, you will be provided with the proper counseling and training to administer this to Drew and he would need to keep this emergency medicine on him at all times. He would also need to wear a medical alert badge so that if he encountered any of these conditions, 911 could be called immediately and they would know how best to treat him to save his life."

By this time, I just sat bug-eyed and dejected. I was speechless. There were other complications of brain surgery, like migraine headaches, that seemed minor compared to the vast, traumatic, medical complications diatribe I had just endured. I covered my mouth. I knew words were not an option. The only thing that was coming out, at this point, was the exhale I had been prolonging for.

Just when I prayed Dr. Heger was done, he went on some more! As he eclipsed the point of ten painful minutes, I knew I was about a minute away from an anxiety scream so loud it would shake the very infrastructure of the hospital. Dr. Heger knew it was a lot to bear. He adjusted his medical lecture style to a more empathic tone.

"I know this all must feel so very overwhelming, because it is. Andrew is in an emergency situation. There's just not a gentle way to deliver this information or a lot of time to make a decision. Should you choose the surgery, we need to get him on the hospital O.R. schedule and consult with the anesthesiologist immediately…"

The decision for me was simple even though releasing the actual words was quite a struggle. I finally exhaled slowly and softly, with my voice cracking, I managed to mutter, "Doctor Heger, please do whatever you feel is best to save my son. I have faith in God. And I have faith in you."

"Thank you for your confidence," Dr. Heger responded. "I will do everything I can for Andrew. I will get you the necessary paperwork and we'll get Andrew on the schedule for surgery immediately."

I thanked him with a handshake. Actually, I just wanted to hug him and not let go. I came out of the office and decided to hug Drew and Jan instead. It was going to be a very long road ahead. I was borderline despondent internally, but externally, Supermom had on her shiny cape, tights, and boots. I decided we should fly over to Andrew's restaurant of choice. I really hadn't eaten since I first received the news the morning before. I didn't think I could really eat very much, but I knew food was important for us all to keep our strengths up, and the one thing I knew about my son was that he loved restaurants with good food! Food was the perfect distraction, as it would help me keep on my best face for Drew. Little did I know it was Drew that was keeping up the great face for me.

Fear Meets Faith

We went to Buffalo Wild Wings. Drew ordered his favorite boneless chicken. Jan did a great job of engaging Drew in his thoughts about what he learned at the doctor's office. Suddenly, towards the end of the meal, Drew stood up and came to the other side of the table where I was sitting. He put his arm around my shoulder and said, "Don't worry, Mom. I want you to know I am strong, and I will be okay."

Hearing him say this shocked me, weakened me, humbled me, and energized my faith all at the same time. I was too choked-up to do anything but smile, kiss, and hug him. I've never fought back tears harder than I did at that moment. What a courageous little soldier God had given me. Andrew meant "Strong." His middle name, Veran, meant "Faith." It was time to stop talking about Faith and start living with her instead! She was a much-welcomed friend in this time of need. I was beginning to see signs that she and Andrew were becoming better acquainted. It made me want to rekindle my own relationship. God was truly at work in both of us.

Drew was scheduled to have surgery on Wednesday, March 24, 2010. In the upcoming days, I had to advise his school of his situation and prepare for him to miss quite a few days of school. The amount of time would be determined on the outcome of his surgery, of course. In the meantime, there were preliminary tests and appointments for Drew, speaking engagements I had to cancel, and family members and close friends I had yet to notify. It became easier to let people know via Facebook posts. The prayers and well wishes came in at an astounding pace and volume. Neighbors, church members, friends I hadn't talked to since elementary school, even total strangers, were all expressing their love, encouragement, and concern.

In all this time, Andrew stayed true to his name, "Strong." I knew he had to be feeling at least a little fear, most likely a ton of it, but that kid did an unbelievable job of not showing it. The only time he actually cried was Sunday morning in church, when he went to the altar and gave his life to Christ, an extremely emotional and spiritual moment that should bring, and usually does bring, anyone to tears.

Drew's father flew in from New York the day before surgery. To take his mind off of the frightening day ahead, we kept him occupied playing games, including a very memorable game of basketball in the driveway. We decided it should be girls against the boys. So, Jan, a former collegiate post player who had only one reliable knee, (the other one tanked years ago to knee replacement), and I, the Hall of Famer convincingly a quarter-century past her prime, took on Drew and Stephen, the greatest trash-talking armchair athlete known to mankind! We had so much fun and enjoyed much needed laughter. There were airballs, bricks, errant passes tossed into the neighbor's yard, complaints of back and knee pain, and excessive fouls.

What truly kept us laughing was the ongoing changing of the score. It is amazing how college-educated, grown folks can't count to ten agreeably. I don't know if we ever decided who actually won the game. That comical argument continues to this day. Andrew was loving every minute of it. He was by far the true star of the game in more ways than one. I have long professed how much sport offers us so many life lessons, grounding us in mental toughness and helping us cultivate a winner's mentality. I knew we would need all of that and more to make it through the extremely challenging days ahead. This was truly a game of hoops and hope.

I've often heard it said that it is darkest before the dawn. However, I now know that sometimes, it is also just plain darkest before the dark. Later that night, I told Andrew he could sleep in the room with me, allowing his father to sleep in his bed, and Jan to sleep in the guest room. Drew went into the bedroom early.

Jan, Stephen, and I were sitting in the family room watching TV when Drew called out for Jan, who went in the room to see what he wanted. After about ten minutes, Jan called out to me to come in. My heart jumped with anxiety.

"What's wrong?" I called out. I had been very jumpy that way ever since Drew's diagnosis. When I walked into the bedroom, Drew's face was shining with tears. He was crying so hard and was so afraid, it instantly knocked the wind out of me. I rushed to the bed and put my arms around my son, rocking him back and forth like I did when he was an infant. Jan began explaining to me that he finally just broke down and he needed his mom to talk to him. I did one better. I prayed with him, assuring him everything I recently had begun to embrace about not hanging out with Worry and Doubt.

We all prayed for quite some time, and I held Drew in my arms that night until he fell off to sleep. I was thankful for his tears, which I believed were not as much an expression of his fears as it was a release from them. Sometimes, we try to show strength to our own detriment. A good cry is a release of so much anxiety and pain, and there is magical comfort that comes from the empathy of others who cry with you. It is a sharing of emotional burden that God calls us to do, expects us to do, especially in times like these. Remember, Jesus wept. I imagined that night, he wept again. It was that empathic thought that allowed me to also fall off to sleep, even if for only a couple of hours.

CHAPTER 4

BLIND LIFE & LEADERSHIP LESSONS

MORNING CAME SO very fast. Together, Stephen and I took Drew to the hospital. We had to arrive at 6:00am. Although Drew's surgery wasn't scheduled until later, there was still a lot of prep work to be done. I went into the triage room with Drew to get him dressed into his surgical gown. There wasn't a lot of talk between us, other than perhaps some restless discussion over what to do with his clothes. Drew was allowed to come back out into the lounge area where his father was waiting. It was there that I awkwardly asked Drew if I could take his picture. I kept thinking, how inappropriate this was, scolding myself with, "The poor boy is going in for a life-threatening brain surgery, and you want to take a picture, like a sick, insensitive, psycho mom?"

The truth was that I really didn't know if this was the last time I would see our son. It wasn't that I lacked faith, but I was preparing myself for harsh reality. I was caught off-guard with Mom and Aunt Delcie. I had already learned the hard way that God's will is not dependent on our desires. Our desires must be dependent upon His will. I had already earnestly and passionately communicated my desires to God that I wanted my son to live. So I now was bracing myself to accept His will and divine order, even if no part of me liked it. There was absolutely nothing I was going to say or do, at this point, that was going to change what God had planned for my son. I put my faith in whatever that plan was. I just prayed that Andrew's living or dying would not be in vain, and that God would be my constant rock to handle whatever came next. I had been humbled to embrace God's plans with the understanding that they were bigger than me and my desires. I held onto the belief that with God, all things were possible. That would have to be enough. Faith was all I had. It was all Drew had. It's all any of us could have. Faith would have to be enough.

In a couple of hours, many friends and family would be at that hospital waiting and praying by Stephen's and my side. I knew that we would be Okay. But at this moment, there was a scared little boy, trying to be strong. What about him? My heart ached in a way that is difficult to put into words. He didn't deserve any of this, and yet here he was enduring all of this. It took everything in my power to smile and try to keep him calm and positive. He was so very brave. He tried to smile. I could feel his pain through those sad eyes. I would have done anything to take it away. I silently prayed for his comfort. After about thirty minutes or so, that comfort showed up in a most artificial and amusing way.

Happy Juice

A nurse brought Drew into another patient care room to give him what I call, the "Happy Juice." This is the point prior to surgery when you get to be "legally high!" I don't mean just a little buzzed, I mean just floating on cloud 9 x 9! It was to help take some of the natural anxiety out of the situation for Drew. I immediately asked the anesthesiologist if Stephen and I could get a dose or two too. He chuckled at the quip, but I was serious!

Within a couple of minutes, Drew was lying on the gurney giggling at everything. It became quite comical trying to talk to him, and in a lot of ways, vicariously I guess, Stephen and I were on the "happy juice" after all! It helped to see he was only feeling giggles and smiles for about five minutes. Then the nurse came in to say it was time to wheel him into surgery. All of the laughter suddenly stopped. I kissed Drew on his forehead and told him I loved him more than anything in the world. His father followed suit.

As they began to wheel him away, I just felt like I needed to say something else, anything else! I felt a jolt of pure, hot, adrenaline rush through me as I stood alongside his gurney! Drew was lying face up, eyes closed, and still half-smiling.

"Drewbear!" I tried to whisper to no avail.

"Yeeeeaaahhh?" He half-giggled.

"Um…Wait! Who's your best friend, Drew? Remember the poem? Who's your New Best Friend?" I exclaimed.

"Faaaaith, Mom! Faith's my new best friend!"

Lump in throat, tears overloading both eyes, pulse on overdrive, I watched them wheel my Drewbear down the hall towards the operating room. Quickly, I turned to Stephen who I had told about the poem a few days earlier, and said, "He remembered! He said Faith! He said Faith!"

With a tear escaping down his cheek, Stephen choked out, "Yep. That's our boy." Even high on "happy juice," during the most frightening uncertainty of his or our lives, Andrew spoke the one sentence we most needed to hear, "Faith's my new best friend." I knew right then, Drew was going to be alright. As for Stephen and me, we held up admirably on the outside, but inside, we both were a complete hot mess! Ahh, but our Andrew, he was hanging out with Faith, feeling no pain and no fear going into that operating room. We decided we would hang out with her too. We headed to the cafeteria to grab coffee and try to see if our nerves would let us digest some breakfast.

For six hours, friends and family trickled in and out of the surgical waiting area of Wolfson's Children's Hospital in downtown Jacksonville, FL. My colleague Lori showed up, to my surprise. Stephen's sister drove all the way in from Tampa. My Aunt Jill drove over an hour from Palm Coast. The prayer warriors were assembled! Time felt like an eternity. It felt so good to have so many people come to say they care and show their support. My faith grew to astronomical heights, so much so I felt like I already knew what Dr. Heger was about to say when he entered the waiting area, looking very tired, his hairline and brow flushed with perspiration, his skin a fleshy hue of rose. I put my hand over my mouth and held my breath in anticipation.

"Andrew did great. The tumor is gone. I was able to get all of it. He's recovering in intensive care. He will need to remain there until his fluid levels are regulated and his vitals are steady," Dr. Heger explained.

The entire waiting room let out a huge sigh, a few "Hallelujahs" and several more "Praise Gods!"

"Thank you! Thank you for everything you did, Dr. Heger! When can I see him?" I pleaded.

"You can go in now. He is, of course, still very heavily sedated, and his face will be very swollen particularly on the right side where we had to operate, so don't be alarmed. His incision is very clean and should heal up nicely." Dr. Heger was always so very direct and thorough. I respected him so much for that.

Awakening and Revelation

I could not wait to get in to see my baby. I know he was twelve, but any good mother knows, they never stop being your baby. I walked into the room to see Drew lying flat on his back. I was expecting to see his head bandaged up in white dressing, something like I'd seen in a movie or two. Instead, I saw the actual scar, a very large scar running from the top of his forehead all the way down to his right ear. His skin had been stapled together by a special adhesive tape that helped to hold his skull in place. His face was very swollen and distorted, especially his right eye. He lay there with both eyes closed. Emotion-filled, I began to softly speak to him.

"Hey, baby. Hey, Drewbear. It's Mom. You did great, baby. You and Faith did great! I'm so proud of you. You're my little soldier. Are you in any pain, baby?" I didn't think he could respond. I mean, the boy just endured six hours of brain surgery. I was really just speaking in case he could hear me, and I needed him to know I was right there by his side. So, it startled me when I heard him softly call out for me, "Mom?"

"Yes, baby, yes, Mom is here. I'm right here. What is it, Drewbear?" I whispered excitedly.

"Mom, I forgot to do my homework." These were his very first words post-brain surgery!

I laughed out loud, much louder than I intended! In the intensity of the moment, it just kind of burst out, "Your homework?" I replied crying from both the laughter and the tension. "I think it's okay you didn't do your homework, sweetie. I'm pretty sure having brain surgery qualifies you for an extension."

I remained at Drew's bedside as his father, and his Godmother Aunties - Felisha, Jan, Carmen, and Monica, all rotated in to see him briefly since only two people could be in the room at one time. At one very memorable point, I was trying hard to be quiet, but I have never been known to display much of an inside voice. I was explaining to his Aunt Felisha how he asked about his home-work and we started laughing so loud Andrew slowly whispered, "Mom?" I moved in close as he very slowly pursed his tiny, dry lips into a circle and said, "Shhhhhh!" With that, I had to leave the room. There was no way I could retain my hysterical laughter, or my unprecedented feelings of tension any longer.

The laughing soon subsided. Andrew was alive, and we praised God for the miracle. I would soon learn, however, that Andrew was also blind. At first, the doctors told us not to worry so much as it may take the optic nerve a little while to adjust. They would come into the room periodically and shine a little flashlight to see if Drew could sense light. It was only darkness.

In the days to come, I would look on with a complete sense of dread. The doctor would ask Drew to raise his hand the second he could see light. Drew never raised his hand. I could see the fear and frustration taking over. "Did you shine the light yet?" Drew would ask earnestly. I continued to assure him it would take time, that there was still quite a bit of swelling over his eyes that could be keeping him from seeing. That was true in the beginning, because Drew's eyes were definitely swollen. Nevertheless, one day, the doctor came in and I could clearly see Drew's eyes were open. He still never saw the light. My son was blind. I was blind, too, because in that moment I had no clue what to do to help my Drew.

Not only were Drew's days in ICU riddled with questions regarding blindness, but the medical team was having great difficulty finding the right medication dosage for the steroids he needed to keep him alive. He stayed tied to an IV that was designed to push steroids that mimicked his natural hormones into his system. The steroid was supposed to trigger his thyroid and kidneys to regularly stimulate then shut down thirst and urination. Unfortunately, they would not regulate, and Drew continued to show high levels of dehydration. Other times, there was too much fluid. He would drink inconceivable amounts of Gatorade and water, and pee by the gallons. It was all very scary. Meanwhile, he had to learn to walk again. We celebrated if he could just make it from the bed to the nurses' station just outside the door. He was so very weak. I never left his bedside. It got so bad; friends were begging me to go home to rest. Little did I know, but I was earning my honorary PhD in Stress Management.

Let There Be Light

One day, maybe about the fourth or fifth day, I was sitting in the corner in the dark. I had a baseball cap pulled over my scary hair. Dr. Heger, who I had seen countless times before, flicked on the light and was startled to see me sitting there.

"I'm sorry," he lamented. "I didn't see you sitting over there. I didn't mean to startle you. I'm Andrew's neurosurgeon, Dr. Heger, you must be his *grandmother!*"

I let out a huge gasp then squawked, "His Grandmother? Dr. Heger, It's me, Vera - Andrew's MOM!"

I had the audacity to be disgusted with him when it was clearly he who should have been disgusted with me! I needed to go home, bathe, wash my hair, and get a spa facial to boot! At 44, and a national television broadcaster, how could I possibly look like a twelve-year-old's GRANDMOTHER? My career, as well as any self-esteem I thought I had, was undergoing serious, instantaneous, unprecedented doom!

Stress had clearly taken its toll on me. I really did need to leave and just try to breathe. Several friends had all volunteered to stay the night, but I just would not leave Drew's side. I was determined to go through every moment, every headache, and every challenge with him, stressed out with bad hair days and all. The grandmother reference was my wake-up call to go home and take better care of myself. I reasoned that Drew deserved and needed a healthy and strong mom, not a broken and weak one. So, I finally traded in the daily hospital bathroom wash-ups and nightly sleeps on a hard, plastic covered bench in ICU, for one night in my own bed, in my own shower, and in my own home.

Early the next morning, I returned and not only was I feeling more refreshed, but Drew was too. The medications and steroids he had been receiving intravenously were beginning to take effect and he was able to eat his first real meal. Then something very special happened. The neurologist came around to do his daily tiny flashlight check, and Drew saw just a little light! I was so excited! Soon after, he could see just a blur of everything that was directly in front of him, including my face! I was so happy that I had wisely gone home and freshened up so as not to scare my poor son to death on his first day of sight! Andrew was totally blind in his right eye, but in his left eye, he could see straight ahead, as if looking through a straw placed in the inner corner close to his nose. He was blind also in the left peripheral. Still, he had at least a little sight, so I saw that as a step in the right healing direction and just prayed that daily it would all improve.

Rehab was tough as Drew was pretty weak and had a lot of pain and pressure in his head. It took his body longer than expected to adjust to the steroids, so they could not let him out of ICU until they believed his body could function with him ingesting his medications, rather than receiving them intravenously. He was getting better taking the daily walks, especially now that he could see a little, but he was terribly thirsty and weak.

By the end of the seventh day, they finally moved Drew out of ICU. The next day, they brought in Tibbs, a seeing eye dog to get Andrew familiar with what may become his future with a pet who would also become his navigation through his new world as a blind or "legally blind person." I struggled with that concept. Legally blind? Could my son ever run the risk of being "illegally blind?" Like, could he go to jail for bumping into people accidentally? Oh, the horrors! I had so many questions. Meanwhile, as Andrew sat up in bed petting his new furry friend, Tibbs kept staring at me as if to say, "Get ready, ma'am. Things are going to be pretty 'ruff!'"

Rough was an understatement. There were meetings with social workers, interviews and assessments with the Division of Blind Services, and brand-new medical specialists Andrew needed to see at regular intervals. He now had an endocrinologist, neurologist, ophthalmologist, allergist, pulmonologist, and nutritionist, in addition to his audiologist and pediatrician. Once released from the hospital, we would spend three to four days a week going back for one test, check-up or consultation or another. Drew would spend the remainder of his 6th grade year being homeschooled. He was often weak and constantly had headaches. He needed to sleep a lot, usually about 12-14 hours a day. He still had excessive periods of thirst and urination, but they were regulated to occur at specific times of the day.

It was a challenge for Drew to walk around, so he began using a cane, although he had not yet received enough orientation and mobility training to know how to use it. He had to begin learning braille as part of his homeschooling. Once a very jovial and outgoing kid, he became extremely shy and reserved. He did not want to go outside and socialize with other kids. He would stay in his room and cry every single day. His emotions naturally bled into my extreme sense of maternal empathy. We both were becoming very depressed, yet still trying to mask it all with a smile, finding or forcing laughter whenever we could.

The Dog Was Right

Let's talk a little more about Tibb's prediction of "ruff!" The very day we first returned home from the hospital I received a call from the landlord of the house I was renting. They said the owner decided to put the house on the market. We had 30 days to move! I almost passed out! I tried to reason with the management company representative. In tears, I explained everything we had just been through. I pleaded for more time.

"Can you at least give us 60 days? My son is not well, and it will be virtually impossible for me to get this place ready in 30 days! We just got home from the hospital!" However, the hard and cold answer was, "We're very sorry, but, no."

The very next phone call I received was from my brother who had gotten himself into a bit of financial trouble. He needed cash immediately. A drug dealer was holding a gun to his head at that very moment and said he would kill him if he did not pay up. I never heard my brother in all my years so distressed. I knew he was in dire need, but his timing, or the devil's, was horrific! I was so beyond myself and not thinking clearly, I screamed, "Put the stupid drug dealer on the phone! Put him on the phone, (expletive!) I just got Drew home from the hospital! I don't have time for this crap, DJ! Are you freaking kidding me?"

"Cis, he will kill me! This is for real! You have to help me now, or you will never see me again.

This is my life, Cis. You are the only one who can save me now! Please!" he shouted back, voice shaking.

That moment turned into quite a fiasco of stress and confusion, far too long to fit into one chapter. So fast forward, I'll just share that the situation was handled with a quick withdrawal from the bank to deplete my already malnourished savings funds, and a thirty-minute drive across town to deliver the money to my brother standing frantic in an apartment parking lot, while Andrew was crying in the backseat of the car.

That's not the only story deserving of its own cinematic script. Once that fire was put out, there was Stephen calling to tell me he had not yet returned to help take care of Drew because his new girlfriend felt "left out" when he came to visit his son for the first three days he was in the hospital. She was upset that he didn't bring her along, and she had insecurities about Stephen's emotional vulnerabilities with him spending so much time around his ex-wife while our child was going through trauma. The caveat was that Stephen said he hoped I would try to see her point of view, and how hard it was for him to deal with her insecurities.

My jaw dropped open so wide, buzzards could have flown into my mouth! So, you can only imagine what flew out! What kind of bizarre, unconscionable universe had I just been cast into? This was all on day number one home from the hospital! I was paranoid to even imagine what day two might hold.

The next 30 days, I focused on the short-term goal of finding a new home for Drew and me. Mission accomplished in one weekend. Then I focused on packing up the home, all the while making sure Drew had what he needed to be homeschooled to finish his sixth-grade year. Having to pack up our home was daunting, but it was also therapeutic to clean out the junk and to focus on a new environment, new opportunities, maybe even new friends for both Drew and me.

Only a month after getting settled into our new home, we made acquaintance with a neighbor who also was a single mom with a son about Drew's age. Deborah and her son, Denzel, were a welcome breath of new friendship air. I was very thankful to make their acquaintance. I began to see a reluctance in Drew, however. He did not have the same energy or desire to make or be around friends. The crying continued daily. I had become tremendously concerned. He was just not the same child emotionally, becoming more and more withdrawn, angry, and extremely sad, no matter how many motivational speeches I offered him.

I often thought back to Tibbs, the service dog, and that feeling I got looking into his big sad eyes that day in Drew's hospital room. Things were indeed far more "ruff" than I realized. I tried to play the role of therapist and fitness trainer trying to help Drew physically get back into shape. Drew despised having to work out and being told what he could not eat to combat his rapid weight gain. I was focused on being a determined, motivational mom who was trying to help my son gain a winner's mentality. Drew was focused on what I was not. I was not the hearing-impaired twelve-year-old with a brain tumor that led to blindness. I was not challenged with a host of body-altering, life-threatening, medical complications. I could not even begin to imagine how hard life had to be for my son. It hurt me to the core every time I tried. I felt so helpless. Every day, it took a lot of prayer and positive self-talk just to get out of the bed, let alone figure out the right things to say and do to help Drew.

Helen Keller Inspiration

One day, Drew came into the kitchen crying. I asked him what the matter was, then he screamed, "I'm tired of bumping into things all of the time! I can't see things on either side, so I just keep tripping and hitting stuff! My head hurts all the time. I'm afraid I won't ever be able to see normally again! What if the tumor comes back? What if I go totally blind?"

On that day, I remember telling myself, "If you don't figure out a way to encourage him right now, you're going to lose him, Vera! He needs your voice, confidence, and guidance, like never before. He needs the strength, perseverance, and courage examples, not your lectures. How do you put a positive spin on this for him?"

It's curious how things you learn in school, things you never think will have much use or meaning for you beyond the knowledge needed to pass a test or write a research paper, come back to you one day. For me, this phenomenon happened in a big way. I remember asking myself, "What on earth do you know about blindness?" At that moment, I remembered how captivated I was when I watched the movie, *The Miracle Worker*, the story about Helen Keller, who was born both blind and deaf and went on to live one of the most inspirationally significant lives in American history. I remembered her quote: *"The world is full of adversity. It is also full of the overcoming of it."*

That was it! The Helen Keller life example was the beginning of the optimism we needed. I had studied her and done a book report about her in junior high school. Rather than giving into the reflex of sorrow after what had happened, maybe it was time to start proactively thinking about how to turn this test into a testimony. Drew was not a victim. We had to trust that God had a plan, and maybe, just maybe, Andrew's story, my story, could have a positive effect on people's lives for hope and strength like Helen Keller's story had done for me and so many others.

Soon, I found myself reading all kinds of inspirational quotes, listening to uplifting songs of faith, praying, and journaling notes, lessons, scripture, discoveries of all kinds to even include encounters with a turtle! (More on that in my next book!) I did not know it then, but I was being primed to begin a new platform of thought leadership, one of faith and fortitude on the speaker's circuit. I would soon begin inviting audiences to "Trust Your Vision and Play Through the Foul." I began sharing what I call "Blind Life and Leadership Lessons." I can still remember the day I wrote them all out. There were seven of them. I had shared many leadership lessons before, but these specific themes would play out in a very profound way in my journey with my son, during an extremely difficult six years of post-brain surgery recovery and development.

There are no fancy intellectual philosophies. "Blind Life and Leadership Lessons" are simple life principles that we all know or have experienced, but often take for granted. We've already been given everything we need to win. We often just don't know they exist; and even when we do, adversity sometimes blinds us to how to use and benefit from them. These specific principles, or strategies, I came to realize, were powerful tools that could help stimulate mental strength and perseverance in everyone's life, particularly in the midst of overcoming life's most difficult adversities. They were too important for me not to share. They are meant to make the very assist we all need when times get "ruff." They are:

7 Blind Life and Leadership Lessons

1. *No Peripheral Distractions.*
2. *Focus on the Goal – Move Towards it One Step at a Time.*
3. *Sometimes, True Strength Means Asking for Help.*
4. *Don't Let the Things You Cannot Do Overshadow the Things YOU CAN!*
5. *Trust You Will Survive Your New Normal.*
6. *One Thing Worse than Losing Your Sight Is Losing Your Vision!*
7. *You Are Significant, so Passionately Play Your Position to find Purpose!*

Whenever I find myself facing difficult challenges, I now

remember and meditate on these important lessons. Much like coaches strategize to overcome challenges to win games and championships, these seven principles are my strategies for countering life's flagrant, blinding, fouls. I write them to encourage you for whatever adversity you encounter. We are so much stronger than we think, but we have to be conditioned with strategic meditations to think positively in order to win. Consider this a playbook for overcoming your own fouls, for finding that way to win, when everything around you threatens you with failure or loss. I hope the challenges Drew and I had to face and overcome will serve as an example of how you can condition your mind to win too.

PART TWO ~ THE LESSONS

CHAPTER 5

NO PERIPHERAL DISTRACTIONS

AFTER HEARING DREW'S pain and frustration over having no peripheral, I decided to offer him a counter perspective. It seemed that all the doctors talked about were the things Andrew could not see, how complicated it would be for him to learn to navigate as a legally blind young man with such a narrow visual field. I understood and appreciated their preparing him for the worst. But, as an athlete and coach, I knew what it felt like to be down by 15 or 20 points at halftime and still celebrate a comeback and a win! It was possible to just believe in the best, have faith, and put a positive spin on the outlook. I said, "Andrew, I know it's got to be so hard, but it's only been a little while. You have to give yourself time to get used to what you can see and stop thinking so much about what you don't have anymore."

Andrew tried to listen and stop crying.

I continued, "I know you have no peripheral, but you know what? You also have *no peripheral distractions!*"

Drew looked on, with those big beautiful eyes. They were eyes that I cherished looking at me so much more after all they had been through. Through those long, black wet, sparkling eyelashes, were two eyes, windows to the biggest heart ever, trying desperately to search me for hope, optimism, understanding, and healing. Drew was such an intense learner. I had always been so lovingly proud of his unique intellect.

I continued passionately, "Andrew, it's like you have a built-in mechanism now to only focus on the goal. Just like in basketball, the basket is straight ahead. If you look right or left, you lose sight of it and likely miss the shot! You only see what's right in front of you. You only see the goal! This can be a good thing! Think about it this way, over here (I pointed right) is Worry, and over here (I pointed left) is Doubt. Just like the poem. Remember? Stop hanging out with Worry and Doubt! God has given you a narrow, fine-tuned window to see through. God is the goal. You have to just focus on His will for your life.

Remember when you were high in the hospital and I asked you who your new best friend was? You said, 'Faaaaith, Mom! Faith's my new best friend!'" I started imitating how goofy he was, lying on the table before they rolled him into surgery. It always made him laugh when I imitated him. This time was no different. He wiped away the tear and belted out a good loud chuckle.

I was encouraged, so I kept going, "Faith is always straight ahead, moving you towards the goal. Maybe you don't actually need your peripheral vision. All you need is what you have. God has given you enough."

Andrew smiled as he replied with a simple "okay, Mom." I think he tried hard just to appease me, but I knew I didn't have his true buy-in. I wasn't even sure if I had my own buy-in just yet, but it sounded so metaphorically brilliant at the time. I knew the thought had to have come from God, because it was true, and it offered us both a little hope. At the very least, my delivery was so comedically powerful, it made my son laugh. I took that as a free throw make. It may not have been the game-winning three-pointer, but it was that extra point we needed at the time to stay in the game. Now we were only down 19 instead of 20. The coach in me took over. I had given him some good, foundational life theory. It takes time for new perspectives to settle in. I, too, would begin having no more peripheral distractions. Worry, Doubt, and Fear were miserable friends. It was time to let those jokers go. Faith was indeed our New Best Friend!

I was determined to focus on the good as much as I could, celebrating Faith who helped us gain the little wins. God had saved Andrew's life. He moved us into a new home when we least could expect or afford one. We never went hungry for a meal. We always had clothes and shoes. While it seemed we were constantly in and out of doctor's offices and hospitals, we had a reliable car to get us there. It was becoming clear that the fouls would keep on coming, but the ability to play through them was as sure as our faith to do so. In fact, it was surer, because God showed up even when our faith wavered.

I began to learn that having no peripheral distractions was more than about having faith and an attitude of gratitude. It was about first recognizing the stress, drama, chaos, and the fouls that threatened our peace of mind. It was then about finding peace in the midst of our storms. So many times, we forget how important it is to calm our spirit, silence the noise and negativity so we can think clearly and make wise decisions. Peace is something we tend to treat as a reaction, or as something that we have to wait to be given to us. We think we have to wait for an ideal time to find peace when the distractions stop. The reality is that peace has to be proactively prioritized, because the distractions never stop. Inner peace is something that always exists, but we constantly have to claim or embrace it for ourselves spiritually.

In a world that gets more technologically advanced, more politically divisive, more relationally divided, and thus, noisier by the minute, it is imperative that peace of mind is our priority. It will not find you. You must go and get it, claim it, and embrace it with complete commitment. To the physical eye, it looks different for everyone: a beach, a long drive, yoga, a game of golf, a sunset walk, fishing, reading a good book, or maybe listening to music. At its deepest state, peace is found in being completely still, in prayer or meditation. However differently we embrace it externally, it comes from the same place internally, deep within your spirit. That's where peace lives in all of us. It is a consciousness of, or connection to our creator, to the universe, to a spirit world beyond our earthly chaos. However, there, sometimes, are places on earth we must go and things we must do physically to get to that place and space emotionally and spiritually. Whatever and wherever it is for you, prioritize it now, because you'll want to know exactly how to find it when you need it most.

Unfortunately, I had not prioritized peace over the years. I welcomed it in the rare, forced moments I could find it, those moments when I became so numb, I had no choice but to just sit and be still. I had reached a point where I had no clue what real peace was anymore. Peace for me, if I was lucky, was when I was sleep. However, there were many restless nights, many nightmares, a great deal of crying, and a spirit that wept continuously. In hindsight, I wish I would have done a greater job of prioritizing my peace, so that it was a familiar and habitual place of rest, not one I severely hungered and thirst for, wandering aimlessly and insatiably in the dark.

I wish I would have understood the repercussions of not prioritizing peace. Like many things in my life, I had to learn the hard way. Yes, I know I stand on stages and seem to have all the answers, but that's because I had caused and had to solve so many of my own problems! We all learn differently, I guess. Friends would tell me that I didn't look rested or physically well. They worried that maybe I should see a doctor or therapist. I know now that they were probably right. But I was too busy being Superwoman. I declared that I had my prayers and my faith, so I would be fine. Fortunately, those were the core fundamentals I needed to move my son ahead. However, I made so many mistakes along the way because my spirit was never at peace. I made emotional, knee-jerk reaction decisions. I was anxious, impatient, short-tempered, and defensive, always bracing for the worst.

Basketball had taught me that playing not to lose was very different than playing to win. The first is coached by Fear. The latter is led by Faith. I was declaring that Faith was my coach yet playing as though Fear was. I know now that part of having no peripheral distractions is learning to regularly lock into a place of peace, where only you and your quiet, positive thoughts have a chance to bond. God has His clearest opportunity to speak and you have your best chance to listen. The key word is "regularly." Prioritizing peace, getting to a place of no peripheral distractions – no worry, no doubt, no fear – takes regular, intentional, meditational practice.

Here I was trying to coach my son into cultivating a mindset of peace, when Lord knows, I was far from an expert. I was slowly, painfully becoming one, however. The key is that I knew what needed to be done even if I hadn't learned how to do it yet. Peace and joy, in the midst of this flagrant, blinding foul were the goals, and true faith was the catalyst to get us there. In order to achieve the light of what these virtues offer, you have to struggle in the dark. The fouls inevitably would come, they already had, with more intensity than either of us could even have imagined. Basketball had taught me long ago that focusing on the foul and not the goal would make scoring and winning far more difficult than it had to be.

Drew and I both desperately wanted to win. We needed to win. We could not settle for anything less than the win. So arriving at a mental and spiritual place of peace was critical to accomplish this ultimate goal. The ultimate goal for all of us, I think, is living a life of peace and joy. I also believe you just don't even think about how badly you desire these precious jewels until you feel void of them. Learning how to turn off peripheral distractions is not something you learn overnight. It is something you learn over life. It is a lesson you do not want to fail. You cannot afford to, not if you want to overcome life's biggest challenges and win. The moment I began learning this lesson, the better life became. It wasn't always easier, but it was indeed better. That alone was a win!

> *REFLECTION: Whatever tough fouls you are going through, before you make a decision, before you make a move; stop. Be still. Breathe. Remove all peripheral distractions of worry, doubt, frustration, confusion, anger, all things that are born of fear, even if just for a moment. Do this regularly. You must become a master of positive thoughts, or you surely will become a slave to the negative ones. Prioritize peace! Become a champion in this area, and even the flagrant fouls will not stand a chance to keep you from your goal. You will manifest what you continuously focus on. So stop hanging out with Worry and Doubt! "No peripheral distractions" means focusing on peace and living in faith that your steps are ordered for ultimate good, thus everything will work out as it should. The goal is PEACE, and JOY always joins in!*

CHAPTER 6

FOCUS ON THE GOAL

AT HIS ONE-MONTH follow-up appointment, Drew had already gained 12 pounds. He began seeing an endocrinologist who ordered him to maintain weekly visits with a nutritionist. I enrolled him in a fitness and nutrition class for kids, and I even took him out on walks, runs, and to the basketball court myself, to try to help him get his strength, endurance, and overall physical health back in shape. Ten more pounds came by the end of his three-month check-up. At the six-month mark, he had gained a full 34 pounds since his surgery. Additionally, the window the ophthalmologist gave us for Andrew's optic nerve to heal and his sight to be restored had come and gone. Drew was fated to live his life totally blind in the right eye, and in about three quarters of his left. As difficult as this was to accept, there was the additional possibility that he would eventually lose even the little sight he had left. There was also the threat that the tumor could return.

Over the next year, I witnessed a child who had been a straight A student, full of love for learning, become tremendously sad and withdrawn. For a little while, he performed exceptionally well academically considering all he had been through. I felt optimistic that he was adjusting and would eventually begin to survive and even thrive in his new normal. I soon discovered that it was all a charade. Andrew was of the amiable personality type. He was a people pleaser. Moreover, he was a mom-pleaser. He just didn't want to say or do anything to disappoint me. What he didn't know is that while he was a good hider, I was a good seeker. I was professionally trained as a reporter to find things out, and ultra-inherently trained as his mother to find out my kid's truth. All loving moms have this super gift, I think. We can tap into it any time we wish.

It wasn't long before I found out Andrew had been hiding the fact that kids bullied and picked on him for being different. They would pseudo-whisper, "Hey, there goes that blind kid." They would jump out in front of him as he tried to navigate the hallways with his cane. "Hey, blind boy, can you see me?" They would try to trip him and call him names or shout obscenities if he accidentally bumped into them. He would manage to escape to the bathroom and cry in a stall until teachers would have to come looking for him when he did not show up for class.

Andrew cried quite often in school and was extremely sensitive to any form of constructive criticism from his teachers. Getting less than a 100 on a test was cause for sobbing. As early as kindergarten, Andrew had tested for giftedness. I never fully understood how much this "gift" had its emotional setbacks. Gifted children are perfectionists and struggle to fit in with their age appropriate peers. While their intellectual abilities may prove to be as much as three to five years advanced, their emotional maturity develops three to five years behind. This reality, compounded with the natural challenges of adolescence, feeling unaccepted as the "nerdy, smart, black kid" with both his black and white peers, he had now also become "the weird, big, blind, black boy with hearing aids," in his mind, to everybody he met. He longed to just be "normal."

Another upsetting development was with his Physical Education teacher. Andrew's IEP instructions were for him to participate in modified physical education. Instead of assigning him a modified exercise or participation plan, Andrew was made to sit off in a corner by himself the entire period. To add salt to that wound, and fuel to my fire, the PE teacher graded Andrew with his first-ever B, not because Andrew wouldn't or couldn't perform, but because he was differently abled, and according to the PE teacher's own admittance, he had no clue how to grade, let alone encourage Andrew.

PE class was just another painful reminder to Drew that he was different, not like the rest of his "normal" kids in class. In consultation with his Physical Education teacher, he told me he didn't want to be responsible for Andrew getting hurt, so it was just better to have him sit out. I bit my tongue so hard it began to bleed. Without regular, physical activity every day, Andrew didn't stand a chance to become physically fit. Nor did he stand the chance to experience the acceptance necessary for emotional security and maturity.

Physical Education class was where Andrew was made to look and feel like some sort of ogre or leper with hearing aids and a white cane. The "adult" in the class had cast him aside, so naturally the children followed suit. The lack of socialization with his peers caused Andrew to feel even more insignificant, insecure, different, and unwanted. There were good teachers, however. Andrew particularly treasured the support he received from Ms. Roebuck, his Language Arts teacher, who watched over him like a mother hawk in school. He also always found comfort going to see his guidance counselor. Ultimately, however, they were adults, not kids or pre-teens, with whom he longed to fit in and just feel normal.

Daily, I would agonize in concern over what I would do with and for Drew. I could not even begin to imagine what had to be going on in his spirit. I wanted to just hold him in my arms and rock all the pain away. However, there was no time for that, even if I could. Money had run incredibly low. The hospital and medical bills kept pouring in daily. I was thankful for medical insurance and Medicare that subsidized a great deal of the cost. I remember looking on in shock the day I opened the hospital bill for just the brain surgery alone. "$335,000.00?" I shrieked. It was the same day I sat down to take care of monthly bills. My total credit card debt was over $50,000.00. I was one month away from not having enough money to pay rent.

I began to daydream, "If just once I could get Publisher's Clearing House to show up on my doorstep. Mama loved herself some Oprah. Maybe it's time for me to hit her up for real!" I decided to take action!

Mama Said Oprah!

Facebook and television had been posting videos about Oprah Winfrey getting her own television network, OWN. She was touring the country running auditions for show ideas and various television hosts. I reasoned with excitement, "This is my big chance! Maybe Drew and my luck will turn around! Maybe this is what Mom was trying to tell me to do - get myself on Oprah! Yes! This is it!"

I packed up my stuff and headed off to Atlanta for my big chance. Drew stayed with Dad for the weekend. I had already prepared my show idea and rehearsed my presentation the entire drive to Atlanta. I stayed with Jan's aunt and uncle, Kim and Tony, who were gracious hosts and even took me down to the site of the auditions themselves.

When we arrived at 4:00 a.m., there were not hundreds, but thousands, of people waiting in line for a number and a stage assignment. My audition would not be until later in the afternoon. I was a bundle of nerves waiting so long. This was my big chance! I could just feel it! I was going to finally meet Oprah! Mom's prophecy, in the midst of my greatest life pain and trauma, was being fulfilled. Andrew and I would have the money we needed so I could get him the absolute best care! I was finally going to meet my idol, and Mom would be so very proud of me. My destiny awaited! The Atlanta event was reported to have attracted far more people than it had prepared for. When it was finally my time to audition, instead of the 3-minute presentation we were all supposed to prepare, we were told we only had 30 seconds to make an elevator pitch.

I was beside myself. I screamed to Kim and Tony, "Thirty seconds? That's it? Just thirty seconds? How was I supposed to get Oprah's people to love my incredible *Play Through the Foul* show idea in just thirty seconds? It would take me that long to clear my throat and say my name!"

My mind was filled with questions and frustration. How was I supposed to tell Oprah's people what had recently happened to my son and how we were playing through the foul and hoping to highlight incredible inspirational stories about countless others who had been through what we had and more? How was I supposed to showcase my great wit and likeability? I wasn't just anybody. I had been trained in television, film, and theatre. I had two degrees and over twenty years of broadcast experience! I was meant to be a star! My mom said so!

In the midst of my private temper tantrum, I remembered all that Drew had been through and how he had to continue to fight. Instantaneously, I felt I could get through this. I didn't come all this way for nothing! So, when my time came to audition, I gave my 30-second personality-packed elevator pitch very proudly, professionally, and powerfully that guess what? I got a call back! I was told I'd be among a handful of people from my session who were advised to wait for a call later that evening. If selected, I would get to return the next morning and appear before a final set of judges to make the final Atlanta cut!

We returned to Kim and Tony's house, but I was a nervous wreck. We had spent twelve hours in mad crowds, nine of those in the hot sun, but it was all worth it! I could feel in my spirit that there was something magical about to happen. Kim kept reminding me it had to be destined because out of all those thousands of people, I got a call back. Oprah's people told me that I would be contacted by cellphone, so I should be sure to stay close to it, as they would only call once. My cellphone never got more atten-tion than it did that night. I stared at it like any moment it was going to stand up and perform tricks.

Hour after hour ticked away. It was ten o'clock when I started getting worried. No call. Kim assured me there were so many more people that needed to audition, they were probably run-ning late. Actually, they never said what time; they just said "later tonight." With that, I tried to relax.

About 10:15 p.m., the phone finally rang. I sprung to my feet and grabbed it without even looking at the caller ID. "Hello, this is Vera!" I shouted, forgetting to remain calm.

"Hello, Cis, this is Dad," my father's voice rang out.

"Dad? Hey, what are you doing calling? I thought you were Oprah's people calling me back." I chuckled not really remember-ing that my father almost never calls me – unless – something – is – WRONG?! "Dad, what's going on?" I startled.

"Yeah, I had to call 911. Drew is very sick. The paramedics are here and need to talk to you. I don't know all of Andrew's medical conditions, so I wasn't sure what to tell them."

The next thing I knew, I was on the phone talking to a paramedic explaining Drew's adrenal insufficiency and diabetes insipidus complications. They made the decision to get him to the hospital and get him on an IV. He was having severe stomach cramping and nausea. His vital signs were heightened. I was already packing my suitcase, grabbing my keys, and motioning to Kim that I had an emergency as I was heading out the door. I hung up the phone and told Kim I had to leave.

"What if the Oprah's people call?" she asked.

Good question. Very good question. "I don't think I have a choice," was the answer. "Drew is sick. I have to get home." I made a call to my long-time best friend, Carmen, who had been like a sister to me since high school. I asked her to get over to the hospital and fill in for me until I could make it back. Kim gave me a hug and asked if I was sure I could make it home. She was concerned that I had to be exhausted after such a long day and almost six hours of driving ahead of me. At 10:30 at night, I would not get home until after 4:00 in the morning. She made me promise I would pull over if I got tired. I promised.

It was a long drive home. When midnight hit, I had to swallow the tough pill that Oprah's people never called. The tougher pill was that they were never going to call. And the granddaddy pill of them all to swallow, was that despite my dreams or even my mother's dreams, Andrew's reality was all that mattered, and was likely all that ever mattered. In lieu of a celebration of being chosen for the Oprah Winfrey Network, I had a party with my girl Pity behind the wheel of my car that night. My tears kept me awake and carried me the remaining four-hour drive home.

Mortgaging Hope

Reasoning that the Oprah quick fame or fortune avenue would not lead me to Redemption Street, I suddenly had a new goal.

I had to find gainful employment. But as a single mom, how was I supposed to manage a job and all of Drew's needs? I didn't have an answer. So, God supplied. Out of the blue, a few days later, I received a call from Tom, a Mortgage Branch Manager at Wells Fargo Bank in Jacksonville, FL. He had heard me speak at a corporate event a while back and was hoping to get me to come speak for his son's football banquet.

I cannot remember how exactly, but somewhere in the midst of that conversation, I broke down crying as I shared the recent turn of events in Andrew's life. I wasn't quite sure how much I would be able to speak to young people about playing through the foul, when all of my recent fouls with my own child felt so very flagrant. I wasn't just "broke" financially, but also I was broken emotionally. Tom's empathic nature read through my pain and met me at my need.

"Vera Jones, I want you in my office first thing Monday morning. I've got a job for you. You're going to be my next Wells Fargo mortgage consultant," Tom said heartily.

I felt so humbled and excited for the opportunity. I hadn't had a paycheck or worked since March. It was now late October. I needed income in the worst way. With the holidays coming, I was ready to do anything. I couldn't afford to say no. I figured maybe this was God sending a financial blessing, and maybe even a new career option.

One day, in March of his seventh-grade year, almost a year to the date of his brain surgery, I received a troubling phone call telling me I should come to the school right away. Andrew needed help!

My heart leaped up into my throat, as it had become accustomed to temporarily hanging out, and I sped off to the school in record pace. Upon arrival, the guidance counselor told me Andrew had another blackout. He was navigating the hallways between classes with his cane and suddenly everything just went black, just like that fateful day playing football in the neighborhood. He started screaming in total fright and stood frozen in shock to the sudden blindness. The guidance counselor was summoned to come get him and escort him into safety in her office until I arrived. I was told his total blindness only lasted for a few minutes. But the fear and the anxiety had camped out and made a long-term home in my poor son's heart, and though I never dared to admit it to him, in mine too.

Excessive and rapid weight gain, frequent headaches, increased fatigue, constant medical challenges and doctor's appointments, and the threat of total and permanent blindness as well as the tumor returning were only the beginning of my poor son's ongoing nightmare. Andrew had to endure bullying at school, belongingness insecurities, and battles with depression, to include suicidal thoughts. He would cry uncontrollably at times, for what on the outside appeared to be the most trivial things. It didn't take long for me to learn that nothing is trivial after a brain tumor, making all other adversity in life pale by comparison.

While I knew the physical challenges would be daunting, I was so very unprepared for the seemingly endless psychological, emotional, and social trauma that would surface. Andrew was a silent, walking time bomb of gloom, pain, and anger. He would try to neatly tuck it away behind his biscuit-loving grin. However, it was inevitable that the emotions would come oozing out, eventually exploding in every direction. Andrew's guidance counselor suggested he return to being homeschooled via the Hospital Homebound program he went through previously, after his surgery, when he was finishing up 6th grade.

Hospital Homebound homeschooling provided a lot more safety and security for Andrew, but it did nothing for improving socialization skills. I would try to get Andrew involved in recreational programs and practically beg him to go outside to meet and play with the neighborhood kids. Each request was met with a coy smile, a head nod, and a return to his bedroom where some sort of video game was awaiting his return.

Tantrums, Trains, Planes, and Canes

I knew my son was hurting, struggling, fighting through his adversities some days, but feeling tremendously defeated more. It had become painfully clear to me that Andrew was depressed and, psychologically, he was becoming defeated. I feared he would hit a point of no return. I think I prayed for and desired his healing even more than he did - so much so - that one day, in the midst of Andrew's crying sessions, I lost all sense of calm and rational thought. Like a frozen Twix candy bar, I just snapped! The baller, the athlete, the competitor, the coach, the fighter, and a surge of the momma-gone-crazy in me kicked in. I went into a mental zone I had never been in before.

We were in the kitchen and he was crying again. After what felt like he had sniffed and gasped for the 221st time in one unforgettable minute, I felt like I had completely lost my mind. "Stop it, Andrew! You've got to stop all this crying! You can't live your life this way! I know you're mad at God, mad at me, mad at your dad, mad at everybody! I know you're sad, and I can't even begin to imagine how hard this must be for you. I can't, sweetie! You've got to learn how to be strong, baby! You will never be able to become who God intends for you to be feeling sorry for yourself every day. You're better than this! You just are! I can't keep telling you! You've got to believe it yourself!" Overwhelmed with emotion, Andrew cried even harder.

"Stop crying, Andrew! Stop crying! I am completely sick of this sadness and depression and 'oh woe is me' every single day! I just can't take it anymore!" I shouted. Then I began to cry, sniffing and gasping for air as tears raced down my cheeks like they were in competition to outdo my son's. I didn't want to cry, but it just happened on its own. I didn't even try to fight it anymore. I justified that it was my turn! I had earned these massive tears, the screaming, the snot bubbles, and the flailing of the arms that came with it! It was indeed my turn and nothing and no one was going to keep me from my tantrum! I had watched my son cry what felt like 1000 times, and that was just in the past month! It was time for him to see how well his Superwoman mom could do it. I had real skills, hidden gifts of pure, over-the-top, dramatic flair for screaming and crying that I don't think he had ever witnessed before, and I'm certain he prayed he would never witness again.

Andrew's eyes were bucked out ten times their normal size. I know I frightened him. I frightened myself. But I wasn't going to end my award-winning tantrum without substance of learning for my child. When I finally calmed down, I marched into my room, and like a manic mommy on a mission, I grabbed my laptop and began looking up airplane flights. I was going to take him to the most congested place I could think of – Downtown, New York City! Yes, Manhattan! Fashion Ave, baby! "Might as well check out Macy's and a few other shops while I'm at it," I reasoned with practicality and conviction. I picked a date in early August of 2011.

Immediately after securing airline travel, I called my friend Karen who had been doing some political analyst work in New York with MSNBC. Auntie Karen, as Drew called her, arranged to get us Broadway tickets to see The Lion King while we were there. We would stay with my Aunt Elsie and Uncle James in New Jersey. I had the entire trip planned in fifteen minutes. It was time for Drew to face his fears, and quite honestly, for me to face my hidden ghosts too.

With his red-tipped, visual aid white cane in hand, we made our way to the Jacksonville Airport headed to Newark, New Jersey. My Uncle James was there to retrieve us and take us to his home. The next day, we headed into the city via the New Jersey Transit. I taught Drew how to read where our destination was, what time the train was coming, and count stops to know where we should get off. I reasoned there was no time like the present for this suburban-raised kid to begin to understand how to use public transportation. It had already been medically established that Drew lacked the visual field requirements necessary to legally drive a car.

When we finally exited our final stop, we took the escalator up to the street level at Penn Station on the Madison Square Garden side. Andrew saw all the people hustling and bustling in every direction. Having navigated the busy train station already, he stopped and looked like he was about to cry. I would have none of it.

"Stop it, Andrew. Are you afraid?" He didn't really answer, and I'm not sure I gave him time if he wanted to. I was in Coach mode. I could see the tears welling up in his eyes, but I was insistent. "There's nothing to be afraid of. Now you listen to me. You're going to take that cane, and I'm going to walk in front. You just follow me, okay?"

Andrew's voice began to crack, "But what if I bump into people?"

"So what!" I exclaimed. "Listen to me, Andrew, because we're not doing the fear thing anymore. Do you understand? I need you to take this cane..." I took the cane from him to demonstrate. "Take your cane like this. Put it out in front of you like your Orientation and Mobility instructor showed you, and just follow behind me. And if people get in your way, so, what! You take this cane and you swing it like this if you have to." I began swinging the cane from left to right like a mad woman trying to whack off people's kneecaps!

I meant for the demonstration to be humorous for him, but Drew stared at me like I was giving him life-or-death Ninja training. I was functioning on a rush of hope-infused determination while secretly hiding my empathic nervousness for my little Drewbear. But there was no time for "Mushy Mom." The Warrior Coach was in full effect. "Just stay behind me and keep moving. Those people will get out of your way! You hear me? Let's go! Auntie Karen's got tickets to the Lion King!" I handed the cane back to him and I began walking down 7th Avenue towards Times Square. I inconspicuously kept peeking over my shoulder to be sure he was right behind me. When he was hesitant, or if I could see the congestion was too difficult to navigate, even for me, I'd stop, grab his arm, reassure him he was doing great, then I'd lead again.

I felt a tiny burst of exhilaration after we had made it through a few long, city blocks of congestion. I really felt like a coach again, pushing my athlete beyond his comfort zone, all the while experimenting with my own. I knew I could not watch Drew forever. He was only 13 now, but one day sooner than we both realized, with God's blessings, he would be a grown man in an oftentimes, cold and cruel world. He would need to know how to be strong, courageous, and independent. In many ways, his life depended on it.

Did I ache and agonize internally for my son? Sure. Of course! But given the risk of enabling him and truly crippling his fortitude for life, pushing him out of his comfort zone, into the streets of New York City, with the guidance of a fiercely determined and loving mother bear, was the best solution I could think of. He was literally learning to walk by faith, not by sight. Doesn't Vera mean Faith? Well, alright then. It was all meant to be! I would teach my son to walk, without peripheral distractions, to focus on the goal and move towards it one step at a time! Back-to-school clothes, a tour of MSNBC to watch Auntie Karen live on TV, and tickets along with backstage passes to the Lion King were our reward.

I was so proud of my son that day. There were a few bursts of emotion here and there, and plenty of fear everywhere else. However, most importantly, there was victory. Andrew focused on a goal and he overcame many fears that day. It is something he has never forgotten, and hopefully you will not either. A time comes for all of us to clear out all peripheral distractions so that we may simply focus on the goal and move towards it one step at a time. No mountain was, or ever will be, climbed without taking that first step. You just have to take it. Period.

Yes indeed, my Drewbear climbed a major mountain, August 3, 2011. He bumped into people, others seemed to compassionately move out of his way, and another one or two people could care less that he was a little blind boy carrying a cane. They practically ran over or through him. Admittedly, a few of those people caught a taste of Momma Bear's sharp tongue and were very lucky Drewbear was holding the cane and not me. I had no problem playing Whack-a-Mole with a kneecap or two, even in hardcore New York! This was probably the most painfully obvious sign that I didn't have all of the best answers. I had enough common sense to know I lacked knowledge and wisdom in a lot of areas to give Drew everything he needed. I wanted the best for my son, and my limited knowledge of how to help him was truly a proverbial case of the blind leading the blind. I at least had enough grit to get us through lesson two, to just focus on the goal of overcoming fear. That guided us to our next very valuable Blind Life and Leadership Lesson.

REFLECTION: *Imagine walking into a gymnasium and seeing several basketball goals. You realize you can only shoot* *at one, so you walk over, and you focus all of your energy there, and you shoot. Life is like that, especially when you are in the midst of adversity. There will always be fouls, and distractions, and multiple goals. When blinded by pain, one of the hardest questions to answer is, "What do you want?" You cannot purposely move ahead without that answer. Taking your eyes off your goal is one of the sure ways to miss that important shot. Being so afraid or emotional that you never take the shot at all, is a definite miss! Remove the worry and doubt and simply decide what's the goal. Once you know, you absolutely have to take that shot!*

CHAPTER 7

ASK FOR HELP

In the midst of the most challenging adversity, you stand to learn some of your most essential life lessons. The greatest lessons are those that teach you some oftentimes painful truths about yourself. I had definitely begun to become humbled about things I thought I, as Superwoman, could do quite proudly and autonomously, if not even self-righteously, by myself. Being abruptly introduced into a very foreign world of the blind and visually impaired was one of the most compassionate and humbling experiences of my life.

There were so many things I just did not know, like basic terminology. An O&M Instructor, for example, stands for Orientation and Mobility. They are those certified in instructions of how to help blind persons navigate their environment, primarily with the use of a white cane. I quickly learned I could not just suddenly know how to help my son in this area based on my own instinct. In fact, if it were left up to me to be Andrew's Orientation and Mobility Instructor, we both would likely end up in prison for assault! Remember I was ready to just whack off the kneecaps of any sidewalk hoarder not willing to move out of the way! Thank goodness, the Division of Blind services appointed an angel named Ms. Michelson to be Andrew's Orientation and Mobility instructor moving forward.

Having endured quite a bit of emotional trauma and stress myself, I also learned I undeniably wasn't always the best counselor. Lord knows, I definitely wasn't the best homeschool tutor. I had already proven my unworthiness flunking Andrew's fourth grade math homework assignments, years ago; something to this day I don't think he has ever forgiven me for. Here we were now, with Andrew headed into eighth grade Algebra and Geometry challenges! We both needed a lifeline, and fast! Oh, the mathematical horrors!

A New Family of Deaf and Blind

Our prayers and needs were answered after attending an informational summer camp at the Florida School for the Deaf and the Blind (FSDB). Ms. Michelson had mentioned the school many times. For the first time, Andrew saw other kids with hearing aids, using sign language. He saw other kids walking with white canes. The very first person we noticed was a cute, little black girl. There was someone else just like him, not just in age or disability, but culturally, too. He longed to fit in and being on a campus with both hearing impaired and visually impaired students of diverse backgrounds was what we both knew he needed. Everyone needs a place to feel like they belong; where they share commonality; where they fell like they matter; and where they feel constructive, productive, and significant.

The summer open house at FSDB was extremely informational. They conducted the three-day session in the perfect way. Parents had their own tract of educational and social sessions and stayed away from their children in a separate dorm. The children stayed together and participated in everything from bowling to kayaking. I was truly beginning to feel that this was just the right fit for my Drew. But I was a bundle of nerves and uncertainty. I continued to tell myself not to hang out with Worry and Doubt. But with all of Andrew's medical issues and being away at a boarding school, away from all he ever knew, at only 13 years of age, truly concerned me.

At one of the sessions in the auditorium, parents had the chance to hear from former FSDB students. As I sat listening intently to each of them and their challenges and successes, I began thinking, "If they can do it, why can't Drew?"

We had a break in the session, and I went to the restroom. There, I met a slender African American woman who was visibly upset. I couldn't help but let my overly empathic nature take over.

"Are you okay?" I asked.

"Yes, I'm fine, thank you," she managed with a smile. "Are you one of the parents participating here?"

"Yes, I am. I have a son who is 13. How about you?" I replied.

"Yes, I have a son here too. He is only six and he has been totally blind since birth. I've heard so many good things about this school. I know this is right for him. But we live in Miami, and this is hard. It's just so very hard to let him go." She began to cry.

"Oh wow, six is very young. And I only live an hour away in Jacksonville, and I'm struggling with this, so I can only imagine how tough this is for you." I tried to comfort her.

"My husband is the strong one. He is the football tough guy. He says we have to do this. Deep down, I know he is right. He just fits in here and I think over time he will come out of his shell, being with other kids like him. This just feels like the hardest thing I've ever had to do. That's my baby, you know?" She cried even harder. "I'm sorry. I'm just having a really tough time."

I comforted her again. "Please don't apologize. I completely understand. I truly do. I'm a single mom, and I feel like I'm stuck right in between being both you and your husband right now. The basketball coach mom in me says, 'Be tough, and help him be strong too, and just let go. He will be fine, and he will learn so much more from people who know exactly how to help him.' But the protective, empathic mom in me says, 'He needs you emotionally. For the greatest part of his life, you are all he has ever known for nurturing and care. How can you just turn him over to complete strangers?'" She nodded in agreement, sobering a little.

We chatted a little while longer in the bathroom and wished each other and our children well. I heard myself tell her that as hard as it is for us loving and protective moms, sometimes, we have to just step out on faith and realize our children are God's too. It's hard to let go, but sometimes, we are all stronger than we actually think. Wow. By trying to help her, I was helping myself. I was beginning to embrace what I needed to do, what really was the only wise, non-emotional, choice to make. Her child, my child, all of the children of the parents here, had to make a very tough decision. The wise choice was actually quite simplistic from a logical perspective. It all boiled down to who and what could help our children the most. Head had to win out over heart.

When we left the camp, Drew was smiling harder than I had seen in a year! He was talkative the entire ride home telling me all of the things they did and how many of the kids were totally blind, but how they still could do a lot of things. They went kayaking, bowling, shot hoops, hung out at the canteen where they had burgers and pizza, and they played games in the gymnasium. He said the magic words I needed to hear - that he just felt like he would fit in there. I asked him about going away to school and living in a dorm. He said he thought it would be fun. I didn't continue down that avenue of thought about being away from home, as I knew my son was a deep thinker and what started as genuine joy and excitement would possibly crash at doom and gloom caused by anxiety and fear. Thus, I encouraged him to keep thinking positive about the possibility of attending FSDB. Meanwhile, I was trying to do the same.

Ask Someone Who Knows

The third Blind Life and Leadership Lesson had become very apparent. I was trying everything I knew to be strong while also encouraging Drew to be tough. Sure, that was a solid plan of action. But maybe there was a better strategy. Maybe it made much more sense to ask someone who knows for sure. Sometimes, true strength means putting your pride aside, your need to have control, and exercising trust or faith in a fellow, capable, and willing human being, or a village of such human beings, as was our case. It means asking for help. Like many of us, I was a very proud person, and in times of stress and tough challenges, I could become very withdrawn and autonomous to my own detriment, as well as to my child's. I just figured I could do it all myself. I could figure things out on my own. I didn't want to ask for help.

In my world, for as long as I could remember, everyone was always depending on me for guidance and help. I was a fixer, a coach, a counselor, a motivator, the smart one, the strong one, the responsible one, the go-to, the go-getter, the achiever. That's what so many people told me they saw in me, and I proudly adorned each of those character attributes like I was invincible. I was voted "Most Likely to Succeed" in high school. I had to live up to the hype! How could I be the one to ask for help? That would make me look weak, right? But here's the irony. Deep down, I was weak. I was beyond weak. I was broken. I was sad, lonely, and I felt tremendously empty, confused, and defeated. I couldn't fix Drew. I was just a helpless, emotionally wounded mother, pretending everything was always alright with the world. Here's what I know, folks: Pretending gets old. Fast. It is mentally, physically, and spiritually exhausting!

When things go wrong, when we are confused, when we are struggling, asking for help seems so very logical, so intrinsic, something so simple to do. Yet this phenomenon of being unwilling to ask others for help is painstakingly common. There are so many reasons why so many people do not ask for help. For some, it's pride, not wanting to seem weak or incompetent. For others, it's caring more about others' needs than our own. We don't want to become a greater burden on anyone else. Then there are also those prominent memories when we asked for help in the past, and our requested helper did not actually do very much to aid us in solving or overcoming our problems or obstacles. So why bother to ask again? Worse, there were painful times when we asked for help and were just told "no" or were rejected in other ways.

If we tried hard enough, we can probably trace our "I don't want to ask for help" dispositions back to some early childhood moment. Some psychologists suggest something simple, perhaps a single incident when we were growing up that caused us to believe we were lazy, dumb, or weak, perhaps for not doing a task we found difficult, could have set the tone for our becoming overly self-reliant, especially if we were chastised or ridiculed for the incompletion of the task. Imagine a child who is teased or made to feel ashamed or stupid for having to ask someone else to tie his shoe, when all of the bigger or smarter or better kids could do it themselves. For me, I distinctly remember my mother stressing to me the importance of never wearing out my welcome. She would tell me to not ask people for favors, and to not be lazy or dependent on others for things I could do myself. She said "God bless the child that's got his or her own."

All of this great advice somehow became distorted in my overanalytical brain and translated into "don't ever ask people for help." It seems so small, but so many things from our past socializations that were meant with the best intentions to perpetuate positive outcomes may be responsible for molding us into this pattern of overly self-reliant thinking. After all, it's a good thing, and it's the right thing, to teach children to learn to do things for themselves. It builds character and it stimulates their growth for the mental toughness needed to achieve, particularly when overcoming obstacles. Yet that pill has side effects, I tell you! It can give you delusions of grandeur and make you believe you are a super-human being who never needs help.

I've now learned, the hard way, when Pride says, "Do it yourself," but Wisdom says, "Ask someone who knows," be sure to listen to Wisdom. Then you can be proud that you did. I humbled up and listened to Wisdom this time. She showed up in the nick of time! We committed to making application with the Florida School for the Deaf and the Blind. We requested enrollment into their boarding program for dual sensory impaired students. At only thirteen years of age, Andrew would have to live in a dormitory on their big campus. Andrew would be housed and enrolled with the blind students rather than the deaf, since that was the more critical of his disabilities.

He was not accepted into FSDB until after his third week of public school. So, he had to briefly return to his old middle school, where he had not been since his blackout the previous spring. This was a blessing because he stayed just long enough to feel confident that he preferred to go to FSDB. It was vital that he was extremely comfortable with this decision. He was excited about all of the new possibilities like learning Braille, meeting new friends, trying new activities, and being shown additional ways to navigate with his cane without causing bodily injury to others like his good-old mom instructed! He would catch a bus for about 50 miles from

Jacksonville to St. Augustine every Monday morning and I would pick him up at the same bus stop every Friday evening. I, surprisingly, was able to get some needed space and time to just breathe, trusting that he was in the hands of people who could truly help him. We spent weekends together, and I'd always be so happy to see him and hear how he was doing.

Andrew's enrollment at FSDB was not just an opportunity for new growth and perspectives for him, but it was for me as well. For the past eighteen months, I had dedicated, what felt like every waking moment, by Drew's side. I had become totally engulfed in making sure he had the things he needed so much so that I never realized how much I had neglected the things I needed. I felt lonely the long weeks Drew was away at his boarding school, but I began doing little things just for myself, like getting a mani-pedi, visiting friends, writing, and taking walks on the beach. Heck, for the first time ever, I even tried online dating! Now you want to talk about becoming more daring and adventurous? That's a whole new book for another time, a multi-genre Romantic Comedy turned Tragedy just waiting to become a National Bestseller!

Ultimately, we all need a little help. Sometimes, we need a lot. I've learned just how important it is to humble myself to allow others to be of significant service. That's actually why we are all here. It is in the unwittingly and purposefully selfish moments of wanting to do everything ourselves that we complicate our own lives. Believe me, we go against the natural flow of the creative universe when we do this. Granted, there are many experiences in this life where we will have to be autonomous, self-reliant, perseverant, and learn tough lessons on our own. These lessons definitely are designed to strengthen our character. I do not ever want to undermine just how important such lessons are. That leads us to the next chapter of Blind Life Lessons; but, I must reiterate how important it is to learn the importance of finding the courage and humility to ask for help. It is a truly blessed lesson, indeed.

REFLECTION: *We must not forget that there is tremendous benefit in being able to recognize when things are outside of our control. Then we must find a level of comfort in allowing ourselves to be vulnerable with those who can truly help. We grow so much in humility, in wisdom, in community, and in unity. We find peace, we empower significance in others, and we just become better. These experiences, much like in sport, are why we are all really here – to play together and to win together. Sometimes, true strength lies in recognizing we need help, and then just letting go of pride, shame, previous disappointments, predispositions, or our stubborn comfort zones to simply ask for it. Do you need help? Will you let go and ask for it? Your growth as well as the growth of others ready and willing to help you, depends on it!*

CHAPTER 8

I CAN

"Andrew is in for a long road. You are too. He is considered legally blind because he has such a limited visual field. If you imagine our full field, to include what we see with a full peripheral, to be close to 180 degrees," Dr. Hered, Andrew's ophthalmologist, rotated his two index fingers from touching each other in front of his nose out to his adjacent shoulders. Then he continued, "Andrew has only about 20% of his visual field. Totally blind in his right eye and no peripheral in his left means there are very few things he can do without being a danger to himself."

"Okay," I muttered while slowly nodding my head as if to say, "I understand, but I sure don't like any of the words coming out your mouth right now, Doc." He was on a roll, so I let him continue.

"When you have no peripheral, it can be very scary to navigate. We can sense when people are crossing our path, as our peripheral helps us to do this. To Andrew, everyone and everything that are not directly in front of him will suddenly appear by complete surprise. This is why it is so important for him to use a white cane or a sighted guide. He won't be able to drive a car, as it would be extremely dangerous for him to merge lanes or to react quickly enough if he were cut off in traffic, or if someone ran an intersection. More than likely, he wouldn't be able to pass the eye test anyway because of his inadequate depth perception."

Dr. Hered continued to explain Andrew's various visual deficiencies as I listened on intently. That conversation played over and over in my head many times in the months following Andrew's brain surgery. Whatever reminders that weren't echoing in my head from that office visit were being played out in reality as Andrew would become frustrated or actually even hurt himself at times as yet another object outside of his narrow visual field – an open kitchen cabinet, a raised sidewalk, a potted plant in the middle of the mall, a chair not pushed in at a dining table – caused him to abruptly stop or stumble, tripped him up, or left him bruised, ultimately proving Dr. Hered's point. It was literally becoming painfully clear for Andrew that he was no longer "normal" like others who had all of their visual field.

It was most painful to Andrew that Dr. Hered told him it would be unlikely he would ever be able to drive a car. Andrew had loved cars since the first time he ever remembered riding in one. Even I held fond memories of being on the floor with him, playing race cars or imagining scenarios as we pushed around his huge collection of Matchbox miniatures on his giant rug with a view of the city. It had a bank, a gas station, train tracks, and a grocery store. We bonded over those times driving those cars to our dreams and fantasy places. Now those cars had become a representation of his growing world of "Can't." His dreams of driving had been crushed. He got rid of his Matchbox car collection at our yard sale a year after his brain tumor. It broke my heart.

Can't Overload

I guess hearing from one doctor about what you can't or shouldn't do would be discouraging enough. But Andrew and I heard it from almost every doctor he visited. It was Dr. Heger, his pediatric neurosurgeon, who first communicated all of Andrew's other complications. These seemed far worse than blindness, with names almost as complicated as their diagnosis. There was the craniopharyngioma itself, a rare brain tumor that affects only two or three children per million.[3] It came with a long list of "Can't" obstacles related to the lack of pituitary function the tumor and subsequent brain surgery debilitated. I can still, even to this day, remember the fear and frozen, negative thoughts that picked fights daily with Hope and Faith, and all optimistic perspective.

"Because Andrew has no pituitary function, he CAN'T produce his own hormones naturally. He will have to live off steroids for the hormones that basically keep us alive every day. He will either take pills or have to inject everything from testosterone, growth hormone, and cortisol. He has a condition called adrenaline insufficiency. Since he CAN'T make adrenaline, if he sustains an injury, like a broken bone or has a high fever, his body CAN'T naturally produce the adrenaline necessary to protect him and react to pain. Therefore, you would need to call 911 immediately. If he doesn't get an emergency injection within 15 minutes or so, he could die."

I gulped and tried to keep my lip from quivering and becoming a tattle tale on my inner fear.

Doctor Heger continued, "So he CAN'T play football or any other contact sport. It's too much of a life-threatening risk. He CAN'T fight through a high fever, so if he catches the flu or any type of virus, it's best to get him to the emergency room the minute his temperature goes higher than 101 degrees."

The lip quiver won out. My fear had now been undeniably exposed.

The endocrinologist, Dr. Gagliardi (it took weeks to remember to just say "Gal-ee-ar-dee" and stop pronouncing the silent "g") picked up where Dr. Heger and Dr. Hered left off with more of what Drew could not do. She explained, "Andrew also has a condition called diabetes insipidus, or more commonly known as water diabetes. This will complicate living a normal life because it will take quite a bit of time to get this regulated. Basically, our thirst and our urination are controlled by hormones. Andrew CAN'T produce this hormone, so we have to put him on steroid medication that controls when he's thirsty and when he goes to the bathroom. Without it, Andrew would pee nonstop and thus dehydrate himself because the amount he would pee out would be significantly greater than the amount he could possibly drink. Andrew CAN'T survive much longer than 2 or 3 hours without this medication. He would put himself in a life-threatening situation. He will likely drink gallons of water daily and urinate in excess of five times that of a typical, normal, healthy person."

There was yet hypothyroidism, migraine headaches, balance and coordination issues, allergies, sleep disorders, prediabetes, excessive, rapid weight gain, and other obesity-related issues, all of which added up to Andrew also requiring counseling and coping strategies for anxiety, anger, and low self-esteem. Each of these complications came with their long list of "CAN'Ts". Imagine being a teenage boy told that he CAN'T eat pizza or burgers, donuts or fries, or drink any kind of juice or soda when he goes out with his friends. Instead, he should opt for a salad, water, or piece of celery. As much as I loved to eat, that would be absolute torture for me, let alone a growing adolescent. I knew Andrew was truly my child, so I realized the least of his struggles – being disciplined about what he ate - would prove to be his greatest! So many "CAN'T's" kept life so very far from simple or comfortable or even enjoyable on many, many days.

Blind Ambition

If there was one concept I began to understand and deeply appreciate from a different perspective by being around the blind and deaf students at FSDB, it was the definition of the word "CAN!" I remember the first time I took Drew to his dorm. The first thing I noticed was a tall blonde boy, walking past us into the kitchen area. I did my best not to stare, but it was amazing to me how, even without his cane, this young man navigated into the kitchen, felt his way around the refrigerator, took out his juice box, then walked over to the pantry shelf and removed a snack bag of chips, then finally returned to the living room area to join in talking with his friends. He was totally blind. He did not bump into anyone or anything. He did not hurt himself. He seemed to have memorized the exact number of steps it required to reach the kitchen, and he seemed quite determined to find his juice and chips. He focused on the goal, he moved ahead one step at a time, and nothing was going to keep him from his objective. The little things sighted people take for granted every day are major hurdles for the blind. Yet they make it seem just as simplistic. It is an "I CAN" mentality and environment. I was intrigued, impressed, and inspired.

Andrew was placed into a room with two other boys. We met his two roommates, once we went inside. One of them I will never ever forget. His name was Trent. Trent was a cute, short, brown-haired kid who reminded me of little Bobby Brady from the Brady Bunch Show back in the 70's. He was a totally blind seventh grader, a year younger than Andrew. Trent heard us when we walked in and politely addressed us accordingly with, "Hey, who is there? My name is Trent."

"Hi, Trent, my name is Andrew Soleyn."

"And I'm his mother, Ms. Soleyn, but you can call me Ms. Jones, Trent. Pleased to meet you."

"Are you our new roommate, Andrew?" Trent asked cheerfully.

"Yes, I am," said Andrew smiling anxiously.

"Cool, man. I heard you were coming. Welcome. Where are you guys from?" Trent inquired.

"We're from Jacksonville," Andrew answered.

"Do you like sports, Andrew?"

"Yeah, a little bit," Andrew responded.

"Cool. I love sports. I watch all of them. I especially love baseball. What's your favorite sport, Andrew?"

That little voice that rudely breaks into my train of thought sometimes abruptly crashed the conversation. "Did he say he *watches* sports? How on earth does he *watch* sports? He is totally blind. What does he mean? This school must be incredible!" Some other part of my consciousness urged the little voice to go away so I could hear the rest of the conversation.

"I like basketball and football, but I don't really have a particular team that I follow," Andrew was saying.

"Yeah, I just love sports, Andrew. I'm going to be a sports broadcaster one day. I love ESPN," Trent said with great enthusiasm.

"Oh yeah?" Andrew joined in the enthusiasm. "My mom is a sports broadcaster. She used to work for ESPN."

"No way!" Trent rose up off the bed with that. "What's your name, ma'am? I bet I know you!"

"My name, professionally, is just Vera Jones, or Coach Jones, but I doubt you know me. I worked at ESPN a long time ago. You would have been just a toddler," I chimed back.

"Do you know Reese Davis? He's my favorite. I watch him all the time. Where do you work now? Are you still calling sports? What sports do you cover?" Trent was super excited now.

"I'm a women's basketball analyst. I work for the Big Ten Network now," I said.

"I know them! I watch them too! I watch them all! Wow, I can't believe your mom is a sportscaster, Andrew. You've got a cool mom! Can you make sure to tell me whenever your mom is going to be on? I want to be sure to watch," Trent said. Then he reminded me, "I'm going to do exactly what you do one day, Coach Jones. Maybe you can give me some pointers or something."

"Sure, Trent. No problem. I will. Anytime." I smiled. It was hard not to. "What an amazing 'Can Do and Will Do' spirit," I thought. I loved it! While I questioned how on earth Trent would ever fulfill that dream given he couldn't see, I was convinced it would happen for him in spite of it. He could hear, and he had so much passion, it totally compensated for his lack of sight. Trent made me believe he had just that much personality, enthusiasm, and "I CAN" determination to make anything happen!

Shortly after that conversation, Tyree walked in. He was a thin African American kid who was visually impaired. He was a bit shyer than Trent. Andrew said hello and introduced himself. Tyree said hello to us both, then walked back out of the room with Trent trailing him with his cane. I felt a surge of emotion. I looked at Andrew and smiled approvingly. I said, "You've got some pretty cool roommates, huh?"

"Yeah," Andrew returned with a smile. "I think I'm going to like it here, Mom."

That was all I needed to hear. A warm blanket covered my weary, maternal soul. I felt comforted. The little voice in my head returned. "Drew is going to be just fine," it said. I agreed.

The dorm supervisor came in and began to explain how Drew would be expected to make his bed, clean his room, and would share in the other rotating dorm chores every week like preparing meals. I almost fainted. She had me at "make his bed and clean his room!" In all my years of trying, these feats remained elusive even when Andrew had great sight. Praise God, my prayers were being answered! She began to explain other important rules and logistics and stressed how their objective was to teach the students as much as they needed to know about being independent and self-reliant as early as possible. At FSDB, plenty of learning would come from classroom studies, but so much more growth would come from personal care and adhering to social norms. At FSDB, they were tremendously aware of what challenges blindness and visual impairment presented, but the goal was to place far more emphasis on what a child can do rather than what he or she can't.

For a year and a half, there was so much emphasis placed on what Andrew would not be able to do because of his disabilities. He couldn't play contact sports like football and basketball; he couldn't easily navigate crowded areas; he would never be able to drive a car; etc. I would always try to put a positive spin on things saying, "Surely, there are other things you CAN do, Drew. You've got to just put your energy into that."

Here was a school that thrived on that belief. It was at this school that Drew would go fishing, kayaking, swimming, and even gain the benefit of participating in sports. He discovered goalball. In all my years in and around sports, I had never heard of goalball.

It is a Paralympic sport for the blind. I became fan number one, never missing an opportunity to get down to see Andrew and his teammates play. I even drove out of town to Atlanta to watch them compete in a goalball tournament. His team was very good. I got to cheer for my child like my parents used to cheer for me and my brother when we were growing up playing sports.

What if every day you woke up, you only focused on what you could do, and just blocked out all of the things you could not? How much different would life be if you rejoiced and celebrated your CANs, no matter how humble or modest they may be to anyone else? It's a totally different perspective, and it is exhilarating. Imagine your car breaking down, and as frustrating as it may be, you say, "Oh great, I CAN take a taxi or catch a bus. I haven't done that in a long time. It may be a challenge, but who knows what adventures or growth opportunities await!" Seems ridiculous or a bit extreme given how we typically react, right? But the blind students at FSDB don't get to get angry that their car broke down. They need to get from point A to point B. Thinking about how they can't do it or feeling sorry for themselves is a waste of time and will never accomplish their goals. Their mindset is different. It is always set on, "How CAN I make this work?"

They Can and They Did

Fast forward to tie a bow on this lesson. In 2017, upon his graduation from FSDB, Tyree had become a high school record-holding track star. The totally blind gentleman I saw walking to get his juice and chips was named Ross. He became a Paralympic qualifying swimmer. Last but not least, my buddy Trent became a sports broadcaster! He is an analyst on the radio for a minor league baseball team in Florida. The first time I heard about it, I beamed with pride like he was my own son. I later caught a video he did not long ago on social media demonstrating how the blind can cook for themselves and various other feats no one expected them to do. It's amazing to see him all grown up now. I get inspired every time I see him, and I always remember that first day we met in the dorm where he told me what he was going to do, because he never allowed himself to say he can't. He knew he could, that he would, and he did. He did not let the things he cannot do overshadow the things he can.

It was amazing to watch this type of attitude slowly take residence in my own child's heart and mind. Each year Andrew was in attendance at FSDB, I realized we spent more and more time talking about his accomplishments, and we celebrated each one with so much more gratitude. I recall the day Drew joined the track team and started throwing the shot put and the discus. I was so proud the day he came home and told me he wanted to get a job. He walked up to the Publix Supermarket, just three quarters of a mile from our home. On his own, he filled out an application. He was called in for an interview a few days later and hired on by the following week! I was so proud of him in his green Publix polo shirt and black apron! He even had his own name badge! You have not seen pride and joy like a legally blind16-year-old with his first corporate polo and name badge! Maybe he couldn't drive cars, but he pushed carts and bagged groceries like a champ!

SPOLIER ALERT! If I may continue to jump ahead for a brief moment, it seems fitting to share here that one of my proudest moments ever was watching my only son walk across the FSDB graduation stage in 2016 as the salutatorian of his graduating class. The emcee announced that Andrew Soleyn would be attending Florida State University on a Florida Bright Future's Scholarship, along with a bunch of other scholarships and awards he had achieved. A young boy, who post-brain surgery, was sad and withdrawn and didn't even want to go to school just six years earlier, had excelled academically. He challenged himself to take advanced placement and college courses to enter a major university with 21 college credits. He had participated in sports and had become his senior class vice president. Above all else, he was a warm-hearted, kind, well-adjusted, and determined 18-year-old young man with a proven "Can Do" mentality.

It's undeniable. There is power in "I CAN!"

> **REFECTION:** *It is just so much better to live life focusing on CANs, not CAN'T's. We all have the ability to do this. Sometimes, we have to be blindsided by adversity to begin to intentionally seek out the positive perspectives we took for granted so many days before adversity struck. We all go through our schools of hard knocks. If we are fortunate, we graduate with our degrees in Can Do Psychology, and our lives are better for it. Also improved are the lives of others, who witness our seemingly miraculous acts of faith and fortitude to overcome obstacles and win in this game of life. Tell me: What can you do to change your life or the lives of others for the better? Focus on that, then make it happen — because YOU CAN!*

CHAPTER 9

NEW NORMAL

WHILE THE LESSON of "I Can" is one of tremendous importance for growth and confidence building, it must be understood that timing plays a great role in what can and what should be accomplished. Even the things we think will be totally awesome to do, come with learning curves, roadblocks, and detours. It takes time, patience, and perseverance to accomplish great feats. It takes greater time to accomplish them when you have already been set back, when your life is trying to rebound from the challenges of a flagrant foul.

While Andrew did a great job of adjusting and excelling on so many levels academically, he still struggled socially at Florida School for the Deaf and the Blind. He was caught in a "Galaxy of Tweener." Many of the children at his school had learning disabilities in addition to their deafness or blindness. Andrew was on the other end of the spectrum, testing quite gifted, with only one or two others on this same level.

In the sighted, hearing, "normal kids'" world, he was different, because he was the partially blind and hearing- impaired boy with a white cane. In the world of kids with disabilities, he was different, because he was the visually and hearing-impaired boy who could at least see and hear a little and he "looked normal." In both worlds, he had become morbidly obese, which brought on a whole new set of physical and psychological health challenges.

Once known to me as one of the happiest, most optimistic kids in the world, with a passionate and gifted love for learning, Andrew had become tremendously withdrawn and often struggled to find even a small semblance of positive self-esteem. He just never felt comfortable in his own skin. No matter how many times he heard me, or others tell him he looked fine, or that he really was just as normal as anyone else, he struggled to consistently embrace it. After all, none of us were blind, deaf, or morbidly obese. We had occasional, "regular" illnesses like common colds and allergies. He had daily, life-threatening disorders and complications and disabilities. How could we possibly know what "fine" was or was not? Our empathy was often perceived as sympathy, making him feel even more different, disabled, dysfunctional, and defeated.

There were days when Drew was extremely happy or excited about something new he had learned or accomplished at school. I would be just as giddy about it as he was! I longed just to see my child healthy and happy. Then there were other days, very dark ones, usually in conjunction with a phone call from the school counselor, Wendy Williams. Andrew was trying so hard to find himself, something common to every teenager. It is something even more common and troublesome to an intellectually gifted teenager with special needs. While much of what Andrew discussed with Ms. Williams was confidential, when his thoughts became so dark that she feared he may hurt himself, she had to call me. I found myself locked in guilt, confusion, and indescribable fear and pain. In a million years, I would have never imagined my smiling, happy-go-lucky, self-professed, elementary school nerd, was now a sad, depressed, angry, and suicidal-thinking high school teenager.

It was Dr. Heger, Andrew's life-saving neurosurgeon, who said to me, "It will take some time, but, eventually, you and Andrew will get used to your *new normal.*"

It was the first time I had ever heard that term. "A new normal? How profound," I remember thinking when Dr. Heger said it at Drew's first follow-up visit outside of the hospital. I took it to mean everything we once knew to be usual, standard, and manageable, or best stated, "comfortable," would undergo an entire surgical reconstruction of its own. What we were left with in the aftermath of this change and adaptation would be the way we would eventually just embrace life and all of the everyday fouls that came with it. What seemed so very unusual, non-standard, and felt very unmanageable and uncomfortable, would one day again, just be a normal way of being, living, learning, and loving.

Negative Thinking

I've come to realize that change is difficult. It is also inevitable. You have to somehow just find the courage to trust you are going to survive it. When you really think about it, every single day is a brand-new day, with an immeasurable array of opportunities and unexpected circumstances that await. The only thing that is certain, in any given moment, is that we are still here. Is it really all in vain? Or are we here for a good reason? Why is it that we seem to embrace so much worry, doubt, and fear of the negative possibilities more than we embrace the positive ones we should relish? Why do we fight change, automatically assuming it will be something negative and destructive?

In 2005, the National Science Foundation published an article regarding research about human thoughts per day. The article stated that the average person has about 12,000 to 60,000 thoughts per day. Of those thoughts, 80% are negative and 95% are exactly the same repetitive thoughts as the day before.[4] If this is true, our "normal" is naturally skewed negatively. We apparently aren't even conscious of it most of the time. Apparently, our brains have not fully evolved from our fearful, pre-historic inclinations to react in fear to everything unknown in order to protect ourselves. The rush of adrenaline, the dilation of the pupils, the heart racing, the heavy breathing, the tense muscles, are all part of the amygdala in our brain physiologically reacting to any perceived threat.

Let's think back to pre-historic times, out in the wild. The dreaded snakes, the menacing large animals or birds, and unfamiliar, outsider humans could prove to be the difference between life and death. Survival depended on man's keen fight or flight response to the unknown or ambiguous. Thus, it has been reasoned we are simply biologically pre-programmed to think and react fearfully to new stimuli and environments. Change, for the slow-to-evolve human brain, is naturally scary, intimidating, and untrustworthy, unless you intentionally program yourself to think differently, positively, and proactively.

Trusting our new normal meant I needed to become more intentional, and more deeply grounded in faith. I decided I could not wake up every day fearing the worst of what was to happen, even if many days it felt like life was trying to convince me I should. I realized I had to intentionally begin to greet the new day embracing change positively and agreeably. I decided I better get used to welcoming it rather than fearing it because every single moment we live and breathe, there is change. When I thought about it that way, fearing change was a bit ridiculous.

In theory, this all made complete sense. However, like most things that involve change in the midst of a flagrant foul, thinking and acting positively, most days, was very hard to actually do. Accomplishing this myself while also trying to get Drew to buy in, on many days, felt impossible. How on earth was I going to get my depressed, teenaged son to understand and embrace his new normal? What on earth could I do or say in such a state of negative circumstances? I never knew thinking positively could ever become so challenging. I never knew my prayers would be summed up with, "Lord, just help me make it through another day. Amen." That didn't sound very positive or motivational at all!

I was becoming exhausted of hearing my own voice constantly trying to share empty optimism and motivation with my son, so I knew he was quite exhausted as well. Everything felt so forced. I was desperate to find anything positive to hold onto. I didn't like this discomfort and Lord knows I was made aware everyday how much it was hurting Drew. I kept looking for this shiny and bright new normal. I wanted huge, brilliant rays of optimistic new normal sunshine. Yet it felt like most days we were in a cold, damp, and dark room with no windows. We just had a tiny flashlight. It was dull, fake light, powered by one small, fading, Dollar Store AA battery. It didn't occur to me at this time that the light we needed had to come from the inside. I had to find out the hard way that forcing your way out of the dark with a tiny flashlight would come complete with a lot of bumps, bruises, scrapes, and scars that would make life worse long before it would get better.

One of the worst decisions I made was trying to force change that was meant to come slowly, at God's desired time. Too often, we are not patient enough to be still in such moments. We want to feel better NOW and no one else's timing will do. There is a time and a place to have such a determined, expedient mindset, but it is not when you are playing through a flagrant foul. In basketball, we used to say there is a difference between being sore and being injured. There is a ginormous difference between minor muscle, joint, or bone soreness, and major muscle tear, joint dislocation, or broken bones. You can play through a little soreness, but you will only make matters worse if you try to push through injury. Injuries need time to heal. I knew this about physical rehabilitation. I did not recognize the implications for spiritual or emotional healing. Learning not to force my new normal may have been one of the most critical lessons I had ever learned – the hard way.

Forcing Change

It was in May, at the conclusion of Andrew's eighth grade year, that I made a rash decision to take a job coaching basketball at what I choose to remain an unnamed university in Florida. At the time, it seemed like the best decision I could make, as financially, things had become very difficult to manage and I felt like I needed a "real job" with a regular paycheck and "real benefits." I missed having an opportunity to coach and help young women grow on and off the basketball court. I thought getting back into the game I loved would get me back out of the dark shadows I feared. Those shadows had hovered since that fateful day in March, two years earlier, when I had first received the dreadful news of Andrew's brain tumor.

Remember my mother told me to give up coaching? She obviously, prophetically knew some things I didn't.

Full of anxious determination, I went to work as an assistant women's basketball Coach under the direction of a young, insecure, immature, first-year head coach. I refer to her as Coach Killjoy. It is important to note that I was not recruited for this position. I sought out this position. In hindsight, I did so more out of fear to find stability, than faith that God had already provided all of the security and stability I needed. Unbeknown to me at the time, was the hard, spiritual truth that I was trying to force my old normal, not gradually embracing a new one. My decision was driven by fear not faith, no matter how much I tried to convince myself otherwise. I wanted to go back to what was comfortable, what I thought was satisfying and secure. I was going backwards into commonplace at a time God had intended to move me forward into a growth space that wasn't common at all.

I missed every possible red flag God could have waved at me in making this decision. I've always found it both sad and amusing how red flags are much easier to see from a rearview mirror, after you have crashed. While ignoring the red flags caused a major crash and flames in my professional life during this time, I had also begun ignoring red flags in my personal life that would cause even greater destruction further down the road. I ignored them because I was trying to play while injured. You seldom make your best decisions when you are in chronic pain. To be fair to myself, I just did not know how injured I truly was.

The painful result was a working relationship with a boss who was intimidated by me, intimidated by most of her own players, and played out those insecurities through passive aggressive behavior. There were countless days and nights that I found myself tremendously frustrated by working for someone who intentionally ignored me to my face and ridiculed me behind my back. It was difficult to believe such behavior could exist outside of a middle school cafeteria. It was painful that Coach Killjoy played out this passive aggressive behavior in front of the players, which caused many of them to resent her even more. It was most painful that the unmerited disrespect she lashed out upon me had such an effect upon me psychologically, that I became more concerned with her childish antics than I was with my own child's needs.

When Coach Killjoy was making the decision whether to hire me for the job, one of the first things she asked me was how I felt about a team that prayed together and if I would be willing to go to church with them. I told her I would and that I found it pretty exciting to be coaching a team that shared that level of unity and faith. She smirked and said cynically, "Perfect. You can pray and go to church with them then. I don't do the whole religious, church thing."

In that same interview, I expressed how important it was for me to work in an environment that believed in family. I explained a good degree of the challenges I faced raising a son with special needs. Coach Killjoy assured me that she was very big on family, given she had a daughter of her own, and that her husband would probably be a great male role model for Drew. I would later find out that Coach Killjoy not only didn't do church, she didn't do family either, except one that I found to be divisive, dysfunctional, and lacking compassion and empathy.

Picking the Scab

In hindsight, I realize so many of those fouls were self-inflicted because trusting in a new normal in the midst of a flagrant foul, means trusting in a process of healing through a natural flow of events that require faith and perseverance. I liken this to when you suffer a severe scrape or cut. Naturally, you do what you can to stop the bleeding, perhaps place some anti-bacterial ointment and a Band-Aid on the wound and allow it to heal. It is sore for some time, and in that time, you pay particular attention to try not to bump or irritate it in anyway. In the "natural" healing process, a scab eventually forms. It's typically unsightly and still a bit sore for a while, but nowhere near as painful as the initial injury. You recognize it is healing.

Then something "itchy" happens. Even though you recognize the scab as part of the healing process, you find it to be a little irritating, itchy, and uncomfortable. Not to mention, the dry, crackling, smashed blackberry on the knee or elbow is not a good look aesthetically. So you curiously begin to pick at it. This is when you open Pandora's scab box. It is in your impatience that you pick at that scab just enough to discover there is a place underneath that has not fully healed. Suddenly, you feel a quick "ouch!" then the scab begins to bleed. Now you have opened the wound to the chance of infection. The healing process must take even longer and could even take a turn for the worse, depending on how much it became infected.

This is exactly what happened to Drew and me when I picked at my new normal wound instead of just allowing it to heal naturally. Raising Drew on little to no income, I became very antsy. The scab became itchy, so to speak. However, neither Drew nor I were healed enough to "force" a major move to a new city. I was now a five-hour drive away from my father, family, and friends, where I had support. Instead of the one-hour bus ride to and from school every Monday morning and Friday afternoon, Drew would have to take a five, sometimes six-hour ride on the bus on Sunday afternoon and return late Friday evening. Our quality time together on the weekends was cut dramatically.

There were so many other areas of our exposed scab that became infected. There was a bathroom onboard the bus, but with Drew suffering from diabetes insipidus, his frequent thirst and need for urination made the trip uncomfortable. Drew also became ill more often and suffered from tremendous waves of anxiety and depression. He was in and out of the hospital on the boarding school campus on average at least once per week. There was very little I could do to comfort him at such a distance. I used to be able to drive down to check on him when he was sick, or even bring him home for a day or two until he felt better. Sometimes, I would simply drive down and pop my head in on him to say hello during the week or participate in parent services events that allowed me to be part of his community of new normal at FSDB. You can never overestimate how much a parent-child hug and a wellness-check moment matter. I certainly did not realize it until the scab was open and bleeding again.

To compound the pain, everything I had hoped to be so exciting and new coaching at the university became very dismal and unnecessarily challenging in all of the wrong ways, for all of the wrong reasons. Coach Killjoy made sure of that. I had heard the term "passive-aggressive" before, but I never fully understood its meaning until I experienced being trapped in Coach Killjoy's menacing, passive-aggressive web. Passive-aggressive people are like little spiders. You typically never see spiders making the web, but you sure know what it feels like when you walk into one, and you surely recognize once you've been bit. Some spiders are poisonous and the venom stings for a very, very long time, causing critical internal damage, and even death if not properly treated. Coach Killjoy's bite came on top of my self-inflicted, freshly picked, bleeding scab, and it hurt in ways I could have never imagined.

There are so many stories I could include here that would leave any reader in bug-eyed suspense and subsequent disgust, but there is only one that I will highlight in this book. The rest will make its way into the most entertaining leadership book ever written!

(Shameless promotional plug. Stay tuned!) This example best highlights what happens when you try to force your new normal. It is unequivocally what happens when you pick the scab off of an already infected, deep stab wound or pull the stitches out too early.

The Madness of March Returns

We had already endured a rollercoaster, losing season. We were an entirely new staff and very diverse. Coach Killjoy's only familiar hire was her best friend, a young, brunette female who was almost a decade younger than Coach Killjoy, and almost two decades younger than me. Let's call her Dilly. The two of them could often be found giggling in the office in one form of gossip or another. If it wasn't making jokes about how our star player played horribly because she was too upset over her grandfather dying, it was making jokes about how we should go to a slave plantation so the black players could learn work ethic, while the white players could stay in the big house. You're looking for the punchlines, right? My sentiment exactly. Not funny.

The gossip and belittling were never limited to just the confines of our team. There was almost always giggles and folly at someone else's expense ready to erupt in our office. Most days, it felt more like a school-girl sleepover than a basketball office. Our men's basketball coach was an African American male and devout Christian, who would often pray with his team. He had a rogue administrative staff member who liked to sneak over to the women's basketball office to share with Coach Killjoy and her bestie how his players hated their coach's stupid prayer time. This would bring the office laughter to volume level 10. He was a favorite target, but still had nothing on me.

For me, coach Killjoy and Dilly saved their best antics. If we rode on Southwest Airlines, where the boarding is based on a first-come, first-served priority, instead of Dilly checking me in early with the A group, along with the rest of the coaches and staff, I would somehow mysteriously end up in the C boarding group, behind all of the players who usually were scattered throughout the B group. So I would typically be one of the last to board the plane. As I would walk on, Coach Killjoy, Dilly, and our older, white male coach, I'll call him Coach Hyper, would all be sitting together in the front of the plane, holding back their laughter that I would have to look for a spot in the back of the plane, usually somewhere in a middle seat. This kind of childish, passive-aggressive behavior went on and on throughout the season in one shape or form.

I had tolerated more absurdity than I ever dreamed possible, learning how to pick my battles carefully so I could just stay sane. I knew the importance of prioritizing peace but kept finding it harder to do in dealing with so much immaturity. I had a son who was dealing with the effects of a brain tumor and I had a boss who found joy in brainless passive aggressive bullying. I was often plagued with guilt knowing I chose to work in this Twilight Zone job while my son was struggling with a lot of depression and anxiety issues as well as major health troubles. He was a five-hour drive away. I felt very guilty.

In my most vulnerable moment, I made yet another bonehead decision to enter into a relationship with a man I'll call Devilin.

There was just no time to date in the first couple of years of Drew's tragedy. I tried a couple of times but discovered many men don't want to date women with children. They definitely don't want to date a woman who is dealing with a child with special needs. My mind and heart were really never in the right place to entertain a new, romantic relationship anyway. Where would I find the time or energy? Yet, here I was forcing my new normal in my professional life, so why not force love into my personal one, too?

Dealing with a passive-aggressive person on the job is absolutely exhausting. When it is your boss, it feels insurmountable, let alone unbelievable. I had figured out the blatant psychology that Coach Killjoy was both immature and insecure on a lot of leadership levels. What I had not figured out was just how deeply her pain stemmed. I had not figured out the lengths she would go to transfer her pain onto me in an effort to shrink me down to size. I had often heard Coach Killjoy brag about how she intentionally did things to "mess with the minds" of various players on our team. She seldom had anything positive to say about anyone that I had observed, other than a recruit she really wanted, or of course, her best friend, Dilly.

I shook my head the day she openly admitted she had just intentionally taken a professional dig at a former employer over some questionable, recruiting and compliance issues. It brought her such pride and pleasure to announce to our staff that she made her old boss squirm at the expense of a player's future. The mean-spiritedness, the passive-aggressiveness, and the overall petty pleasures Coach Killjoy performed, seemed to know no limit. I wanted out so very badly. It took only three months of observation to know I had made a horrible decision in taking the job. Still, I worked as hard as I could hoping things would eventually get better once we were all more comfortable with each other as a brand-new staff.

By the six-month mark, at the beginning of the basketball season, things had only gotten worse. I had invested in an entire move and relocation to take the job, and although I was receiving a regular paycheck and medical benefits, I was still just getting by financially. I felt trapped. Coach Killjoy was becoming more and more unbearable. Still, I just didn't see how I could uproot and move my son again. We had no place to go. I owned a condo in Jacksonville, FL but I had rented it out through the end of June. It was just December. The season would end in March. Where would I go? What other job could I find? This new normal was anything but normal! It was torture. I had never been so unhappy or felt more professionally suffocated. I prayed for freedom.

Along came March Madness, the month I had always dreaded. It was the anniversary month of my mother's fatal heart attack. It was the anniversary month of my son's brain tumor diagnosis and surgery. It was the month in coaching basketball that almost always ended with a loss. I could feel the ominous clouds beginning to hover again when I received yet another dreaded overnight phone call about 2:30 am. It was my father. Drew had stayed with him in Jacksonville, Florida for the weekend as I was out of town at our conference tournament way off in Little Rock, Arkansas. He had to call 911 to get Drew to the hospital. They did not know what was wrong yet, but I needed to come home quickly.

Quickly? How possible was that? It was the middle of the night! I was over 800 miles away! I knew nothing about Little Rock. How far was the airport? How would I find a flight this time of night and how much would it cost? My heart was racing so fast I could barely breathe. I couldn't think straight. Our team had just lost in the first round earlier in the day. We would be flying back to Florida sometime in the afternoon. But that would be way too late! It was still a five-hour drive for me once we finally landed! I had to find the first flight out right now. There was no other way and no time to waste! I grabbed my cellphone. Every thought was isolated, meticulous, and rapid:

- *Google. Search.*
- *Orbitz.com.*
- *Flight search.*
- *Little Rock to Jacksonville.*
- *Sort by earliest flight.*
- *5am, Delta Airlines, connecting flight, arrives Jacksonville 12:00 pm-ish.*
- *Select. Cost?*
- *$1074.00! What?!! Sheesh!!*
- *No choice! Book it! Now! Praise God for a credit card with room on it!*

Next, I jumped up, brushed my teeth, and took the fastest shower ever recorded. I threw everything in my suitcase. My heart was still racing, and my head was throbbing. I called down to the front desk to arrange a taxi pickup. They said they could have one ready in 15 minutes. Perfect. If I rushed, I could make it. I had to make it!

I arrived at the airport about 3:30 am. My head was spinning. I called my father to tell him my flight arrangements. I texted one of my besties, Carmen, to see if she could pick me up from the airport when I landed and also get over to the hospital at her earliest convenience to run medical interference for me until I could get there. I was shaking with fear and anxiety. In all of this, I actually struggled with when and how I was going to tell Coach Killjoy.

For so long, Coach Killjoy had made me feel so self-conscious about performing my coaching duties. Anytime I had to tell her about anything I had to do with my son, there was a sigh and an eye roll. She had a healthy daughter, and a husband at home to look after her. There was just no way to get her to understand the struggles I faced as a single mother of a special-needs son. To her, I was a slacker, with a victim mentality, making excuses for not adequately performing my coaching duties. I never requested to be removed from my responsibilities and often suggested other things I would or could do to make up for any inconvenience his medical care or needs may have caused. Her lack of compassion for my situation often made me secretly wish that just once she would have to walk a day in my maternal shoes. I sacrificed a lot trying to prove I belonged to a woman who lacked emotional intelligence and empathic leadership, two areas that were my absolute strengths. I was guilty of expecting her to react the way I would have. I was always disappointed.

I waited until I was about to board the plane, about 4:30am, to send my text. I did not want to wake her up, but I also did not want her to wake up expecting me to be at the hotel with the team and not see me. I explained everything I had gathered about Drew's emergency situation in the best, most concise detail I knew how. I could already feel her rolling her eyes and judging me as being problematic. Coach Killjoy failed to realize that not only was I Drew's mother, but also one of the most valuable assets I brought to our team was an emotional connection to our players. Unappreciated by her was the fact that I was also the trusted ear for the various psychological and personal issues a few of our players were facing, such as relationship issues, rape, anxiety, and depression, as well as those who felt intimidated or bullied by Coach Killjoy. I spent so much time trying to quietly put out so many fires behind the scenes, I was emotionally drained far more than she realized or respected.

It all came pouring out of me as I sat on that plane. I could not control the tears another moment. Lack of sleep and extreme, emotional stress overload didn't help. I had no idea what was wrong with Drew. I didn't even know if my son would even be alive when I landed. His adrenal insufficiency was always so frightening to me. He had diarrhea and vomiting, and he was lethargic and could barely walk or move. What was happening? I was so very scared. I had to just trust God.

On the plane, I thought about all I had sacrificed to take this job that Coach Killjoy assured me prior to acceptance would be so very fun and family-oriented in nature. It was the job she said I would be counted on to have a connection to the players, because she admittedly was more of an introvert. She didn't like emotional drama. She once told me no one plays the victim more than these entitled kids, especially the black ones.

"Black women are the worst. No one plays the victim more than black women," she snarled.

My mouth dropped in shock as I quickly gave her my opposing viewpoint along with my disapproval of her offensive comment. Apparently, Coach Killjoy concocted this viewpoint from her previous working years in the department of corrections where the inmates were mostly black women who tried to disrespect her because she was bi-racial. She said they thought since she was so fair-skinned, she would be easy to push over. She laughed smugly when she told me she was their worst enemy. The biggest compliment she received was being called "Queen Bitch." I remembered telling her, "Yeah, but this isn't prison. These kids aren't in jail. They are college athletes looking to women like you and me to mentor them, not subject them to greater racial stereotypes. It's that mindset that is the problem." I should have brought in my son's hearing aids for that conversation as my words definitely fell on deaf ears.

Guilt, Pain, and Shame

The tears kept pouring down my face. I had put up with so much crap. My son had put up with so much crap. I truly didn't know what normal was anymore. Life felt lonely, miserable, and confused. The guilt was too much to bear. I caused this. I made this dumb decision and took this job! "Drew, I am so sorry!" I thought about how the young, black male coach, I'll call him Coach Flit, on our staff had pulled me aside a few times when no one was around. He told me he felt sorry for me because it was obvious Coach Killjoy had it in for me – for no reason that he could understand.

He said, "She is jealous of you. I think she feels threatened because the kids love you. They always pop their head into your office, but you notice they don't even go near her door. They hate her! I feel bad for you. It's not right, but I don't even come around you a lot of times because she is so petty, I'm afraid she is going to think you and I are in a clique against her. I don't think she likes seeing the black coaches or the black players together. I'm afraid she will start treating me like she treats you! So I just keep my distance."

Instead of a trusted leader, I had become Coach Killjoy's despised leper. All of this was the price I had paid for forcing my new normal. With that thought pounding in my head, I just let the tears carry me off to sleep. I had a layover and then another flight to get me to Jacksonville to get through. I needed to be rested to face whatever lay ahead.

Carmen was there to pick me up in Jacksonville and speed me off to the airport. Drew was in intensive care when I arrived. Choking back tears, I did the strong mom thing, always ready with a joke to get him to smile.

"Boy, you sure do know how to get attention!"

"Hi, Mom."

I could tell he was so very relieved to see me.

"Hi, baby. How are you feeling?" I asked.

"Just tired. Weak," Drew replied as he rolled his head off to the side to fall back to sleep.

"Ok, sweetie, get some rest. I'm here now. We are going to find out what's wrong and get you fixed up soon, Okay?"

"Ok." He slept peacefully.

Andrew had contracted some sort of virus. Due to his adrenal insufficiency and diabetes insipidus as well as his hyperthyroidism, it was difficult to regulate all of his hormones and fluids. He was extremely dehydrated. It was very similar to what he experienced when he first came out of brain surgery three years earlier. They would need to continue to make adjustments to all his steroids and fluids to regulate all of his endocrine levels. They also needed to get his fever down. He would need to remain in ICU until they felt comfortable that he could sustain himself without intravenous fluids.

I slept in the hospital by Drew's side just like I had post-brain surgery. It was me, however, who I thought needed brain surgery. I needed a wise, functional replacement. Mine clearly had not been working right to put so much unnecessary strain on myself, on Drew, and even on my father. It was plain and simple. I never should have moved away. The universe was teaching me a lesson. I irritated the wound, picked at the scab, and now everything was bleeding, infected, and painful all over again. I was worn-out, defeated, and exhausted. I'm not sure the universe cared, however. It clearly had a bit more teaching to do.

The Terminator

It was a Saturday when I flew home from Little Rock. On Monday morning, I received a group email from Coach Killjoy. It explained that everyone must be back in the office on Wednesday for a mandatory, full athletic department staff meeting. In addition, we would have women's basketball staff evaluations. I had reached out to explain to Coach Killjoy that my son was still in the hospital. She had not even inquired how he was doing. She simply said the meetings were mandatory. So I made arrangements to rent a car for Tuesday evening to get myself back. I stayed as late as I could into Tuesday evening to maximize my time with Drew. It broke my heart that I had to leave him in the hospital, as he was still not strong or well enough to go home with me. He did not get out of the hospital until Wednesday. My 84-year old father was there to discharge him and drive him safely back to his boarding school.

Meanwhile, my Wednesday was shaping up to be one for the history books. After making the long drive back to home late Tuesday night, I woke up quite exhausted with a very heavy heart. My mind was full of anxieties, anger, and confusion. I was sad about my son and all he had been through. I was enraged with Coach Killjoy's childish antics and all she had put me through. I drove into work praying every mile of the way for peace and tolerance. I put on my usual smile as I walked into the office. Only our young black male coach cared enough to ask me how Drew was doing. Coach Killjoy never even manifested a good morning. She obviously knew something I didn't. Good was not a part of the plan.

We went off to attend the all-department meeting. At the end, the athletic director held a raffle. The prize was a two-night stay at a local Hilton hotel which sat on the ocean. It was the craziest thing, as I very seldom ever win raffles, casino jackpots, or any games of chance, but this day was my lucky day! They called out the final four numbers on the tickets. I looked down at the tiny red stub in my hand. "Bingo!" I yelled out to the laughter of my colleagues. I was so very excited as I rushed up to the front of the room to claim my prize. A mini staycation at the oceanfront Hilton! Whoo hoo! I was so excited!

I looked up from the envelope the AD handed me and caught a glimpse of Coach Killjoy. She was looking directly at Dilly. They both smirked at each other as if they knew something I didn't. I would soon find out the big secret. We returned to our women's basketball office after the meeting and Coach Killjoy began holding the closed-door evaluation meetings she had emailed us about. My meeting was saved for last. I watched as my other three colleagues entered and exited with papers in their hand, like little report cards of their performances. Each session seemed to last about twenty to thirty minutes. So a little over an hour and a half had passed when it was my turn to go into her office.

"Close the door, please," Coach Killjoy said softly.

I obliged, then took my seat on the other side of her large desk directly facing her.

"So how is Drew doing?" she inquired.

It caught me off-guard. In everything that had happened, from me leaving Little Rock abruptly in the middle of the night; sharing with Coach Killjoy that he was in intensive care; leaving him in the hospital to drive all the way back to work; this was the first and only time she had asked about my child's well-being. I had grown accustomed to her just not giving a frog's fart, so I was indeed quite startled at what should have been a commonplace, empathic gesture of goodwill.

"He's hanging in there. My father will hopefully bring him home from the hospital today. I had to leave before he was released," I responded with a raised eyebrow. Her intentions just didn't seem pure. I knew better.

With no other response on that topic, she asked, "So tell me your thoughts on our season. How do you think things went?"

"Wow! Enough of the small talk, let's dive right in the deep end, why don't we?" I sat upright in my chair, took a deep breath, and just poured out my truth. I began with things strictly related to basketball, our wins and losses, the morale of the team, the things I believed she wanted to hear. She was not one for emotional per-spectives, so I kept pouring out the facts and data, X's and O's I thought she desired.

When I was done, she said, "No, I mean, how do you feel about you and me?"

Again, I was caught off-guard. Several times throughout the season, I had tried to open this door. I'm a communication professional. I train on empathic leadership, and I believe in team-building, staff comradery, cohesiveness, and all things relationally positive. Every time I had tried to bridge the obvious gap in our core val-ues, our personality styles, and our obviously dysfunctional work-ing relationship, I was met with aloofness or denial that there was anything to be concerned about. Today, suddenly she wanted to talk about my feelings? Interesting. Well, the truth shall set you free, right?

She wanted truth, so truth I gave her. I explained that I did not feel respected and struggled with always feeling like I was an outsider and the butt end of her and Dilly's jokes. I felt belittled in front of the players. I felt that no matter how much I went above and beyond to win her approval it was a losing battle as she had already seemed to predetermine my unworthiness. I told her I had tried on countless occasions to get on the same page with her. It was my only desire to be the best assistant to her I knew how to be. I related back to when she told me she needed a strong voice, and I quote, "a strong black woman's voice," that the players would listen to and respect. I told her I gave her just that, but it seemed my voice and connection to the players turned out to be the very thing that she resented.

With this she interjected, "Well, it's like after a while, they only wanted to listen to you."

In my mind, I was thinking, "Because you have the personality of a stick and the compassion of a stone, and your words are very hurtful." But I chose to engage her differently. "Well, you asked me about what my feelings were. You are the head coach, so I suppose this meeting is really about what your feelings are. I don't actually see a written evaluation, so my guess is that you have some things you wish to share." I was at the farthest extent of diplomacy I could muster. I could already see the writing on the wall, and there weren't any nice words involved.

My armpits began to sweat, and I could feel the lump growing in my throat as she coyly said the words I'll never forget in a tone I can't un-hear, "I just think we need to move in another direction." I had always heard about this diplomatic statement and had even coached an executive or two to use it in the past. Here I was on the receiving end of the most polite and tactful way of saying, "You're no longer wanted or needed here. You're fired."

With this statement, Coach Killjoy turned white as a ghost like it frightened her more to say it than for me to hear it. I didn't let her off that easy because at this point I was pissed off beyond measure. I could actually see myself leaping across her big desk and choking the daylights out of her. (I knew it wasn't Christian, but it's even less Christian to lie about it.) I chose to engage her in further conversation instead.

"So you are firing me, Killjoy? Is that what this is? You brought me all the way back here, leaving my son in the hospital for a mandatory evaluation, yet you sit here with no evaluation papers anywhere, and you want to suddenly play 'let's talk about our feelings?' Yes, let's talk about them!" I had lost all cool points, as my calm demeanor had just undergone major cosmetic surgery. "What exactly is this new direction, Killjoy? You mean you're firing me?"

She looked tremendously uncomfortable, like when you get a gas bubble on a crowded airplane. "Well, no, I'm not saying that, I mean I would want you to at least finish out the year and maybe just resign. I mean you don't have to leave right away," she rambled on.

"I don't get it," I interrupted. "Either you are firing me or you're not. Since you won't be clear, let me be clear. I'm not quitting. I lost money uprooting my son to move all the way down here. Now you want me to peacefully resign and move myself all the way back? I don't have anywhere to move to, Killjoy! But you know what, it's fine because I've had enough of the passive-aggressive giggles, racist jokes, pettiness, and your insensitivity to my son. You told me working here would feel like family. This hasn't been a family. I don't know what you consider family, but it sure isn't the way you have treated me and my son."

A voice kept saying "don't say too much, Vera, just bow out gracefully," but it was no match for the Leo pride that took over or the exhaustion and disgust and resentment I had carried around for months. It was time to let it all out. I had absolutely nothing to lose. She was teary-eyed now trying to explain her point of view. I had hit a nerve when I talked about family. That was her sore spot. I believe somewhere in that dark exterior, there was an interior conscience that knew she was guilty of treating us the way she did and here she was now trying to justify it all while asking me to leave quietly instead of finding the guts to just officially terminate me.

"So when is my last day, Killjoy? Today? Is today my last day?"

"Well, no....Um, I don't know." She was truly rattled.

"Well, if I'm fired, I'm going to pack my stuff now. I'm not quitting. If I quit, I can't get unemployment. I have a son to take care of, Killjoy. I have to find a place to live. I'll have no income. So you'll have to fire me. I'm not quitting," I shot back.

Now Coach Killjoy was the one who was caught off-guard. She just figured I would bow out gracefully.

"Well, wait. I need to go talk to (my boss). I don't know what day will be your last day. I....I...I'm not sure. I don't know how this works. You don't have to come in anymore. I will talk to (my boss) and I will let you know what's next."

It really didn't matter what was next. I had never been fired, or forced my own firing, as it were. I had to do the walk of shame out her office as Dilly looked on with a smirk then tried to look away. I had been shouting and my voice was already on the loud side, so I knew everyone had heard the bulk of what happened. I didn't care. I was so tired. So defeated. So devastated. I just wanted peace. I just wanted that freedom I prayed for. I realized God had delivered. It wasn't pretty, but I got what I asked for. I got what I needed. I grabbed my laptop backpack and headed out the door, preserving my cry for the drive home.

I opted to use my oceanfront Hilton staycation right away. I would spend the next two days on the beach with my boyfriend, Devilin, who I had to convince not to drive over and blow up Coach Killjoy's office. I would reflect, vent, cry, laugh, and drink fruity drinks with little umbrellas. I exhaled. I allowed myself to think about all of the lessons that came with trying to force my new normal. They were extremely painful lessons. I learned them the hard way and I had no interest in ever having to repeat this nine-month course. I had fully picked off the scab. It had become infected and bled for a very long time.

Sitting on my hotel balcony, looking out over the water, I took in the healing power of the sun. It was shining with a most-gentle March breeze. My pride was hurt, but my spirit was free again. God had my full attention now. A new and improved normal was predestined for me, but this time I knew how to leave the scab alone, and just let it heal naturally. I vowed I was done forcing my new normal – hopefully forever.

> **REFLECTION:** *One of the many definitions of normal is "occurring naturally." If this holds true, then forcing your new normal is very unnatural. Going against that which is natural will always yield unfavorable consequences, especially when you are trying to heal emotionally and spiritually. Human beings are resilient. Human beings who walk in faith are even more so! We have been created to adapt to some of the most incredulous circumstances, but all things evolve in time. Do you ever underestimate the importance of just being still, trusting in God's will, and taking life slowly when you are trying to heal from a major life challenge? Trust that, eventually, you will learn to thrive in your new normal. Don't fear it and don't force it. Everything will work out as it should.*

CHAPTER 10

SIGHT vs. VISION

ON JULY 1 of 2013, I returned home to my condo in Jacksonville, FL. I remained in limbo at the university, not knowing what my actual date of dismissal was for almost two months. It was unsettling but at least I continued to receive a paycheck until May, even though I had not worked since March 13th. No matter how much I agonized about it, I was jobless again, and for the first time in my life, I felt unwanted and not valued. I was broke and broken. I had to start over. My choice was to move back to Jacksonville, Florida – back home. Home is where I never should have left.

Walking into my condo for the first time in a year, a wave of gratitude filled my spirit. The very security I went searching for was here all along. The grass was far greener here than I ever knew. It took a romp in the mud to appreciate it.

No Place like Home

I began to reflect on how miraculously this condo came to be home. As I mentioned earlier, in March of 2010, directly after Drew's brain surgery, we were given the unexpected 30-day notice that our rented home would be sold. I found a new house to rent on the west side of town. By October of 2010, Drew's medical bills were piling up. My last paycheck had come in February from my seasonal work with BTN. I had maxed out every credit card. My bank account indicated I had just enough money left to pay November's rent and utilities. Countless times, at what felt like the last possible moment, God had just miraculously shown up and fulfilled our every need. This time, however, it seemed like God was really busy, or maybe, much like my bank account, my miracles were also scarce.

Despair welled up in my already overly taxed eyes. I was a blink away from a facial waterfall when my cellphone rang. This was that fateful day when Tom, the Wells Fargo Mortgage Branch Manager, called me about coming to speak at his son's football banquet. The next thing I knew, I had a job as a mortgage consultant.

I knew absolutely nothing about mortgage consulting except that I had purchased a few homes previously, and I had an idea of the process from the customer's viewpoint. My mother had been a banking professional, and my father an architectural engineer. I loved homes and had previous experience as a real estate agent. I had worked in corporate and media sales a few decades prior. That was the best I could come up with for qualifying myself for that position. As far as Tom was concerned, I was qualified. He said I was a baller, so he knew I had a winner's mentality. As far as I was concerned, I was struggling financially and as close to desperate as I could be without losing all of my dignity. So I eagerly and gratefully showed up Monday morning and accepted that position. Most importantly, I guess, God knew I was qualified and once again He provided and prevailed.

Unexpectedly, there I was, a Wells Fargo Mortgage Consultant. Tom turned out to be one of the best bosses I had ever worked for. He was a true empathic leader, who embodied many of the principles I use in my leadership training and coaching today. He was a far cry from Coach Killjoy, that's for darn sure! It was because of the relationships and knowledge I gained in my brief period of employment with Wells Fargo Bank, that I began to find out about various sale properties, including foreclosures in the area. That blessing just came to me. I didn't have to force anything.

In March of 2011, I discovered a 3-bedroom, 2-1/2 bath townhouse in great condition. I decided to step out on faith and take what felt like a huge risk. Years ago, I had put away money in an annuity for retirement. I had never touched it and, for the most part, I purposely forgot all about it, as I never wanted to be tempted to spend it up on cute shoes or any of the other frivolous temptations that always found amusement in taunting me. I had very little other savings, so cashing out this annuity was the biggest financial risk I had ever taken. But I took it. For the first time ever, I bought a home with cash. There was a calm when I made this purchase. I felt God say, "I am providing you a place to call home with no worries over a mortgage or how you will keep a roof over your head."

Only one year later, the very security I needed, the very dressing necessary to keep the wound covered, if we return to my scab analogy, I chose to remove. God provided us with mortgage-free home ownership. We were already beginning to transition into our new normal. We were healing. Yet, under that covering, the ugly scab began to itch, so I chose to remove it. I thought it would heal faster if I came up with a new remedy. Barely in the home for a year, I rushed the natural healing process God had intended. Why? Because, clearly, I was impatient, and obviously not very bright. I had a home, but I had no "regular job" or "normal stability" and I became fearful that with Drew's health conditions, the itchy, ugly scab might get worse, so I felt impelled to pick it. I traded peace for panic, and faith for fear.

Home. It felt so good to be back. That may have been the only true light I could find in the aftermath of the dark hole I had dug for myself trying to force a "new normal" that I thought would make me comfortable. Basketball. Coaching. A regular paycheck with benefits. That was what I had grown used to. But if this was the "old normal," how on earth could I have expected it to be the new one? Little aha moments of profound, albeit painful, truths were becoming daily revelations. These Blind Life and Leadership Lessons were beginning to become more apparent, and yet, class had just come into session on what I found to be the most profound of all lessons.

Profound Perspective

In what some would call a twist of fate, but what I know to be divine intervention, a colleague named Lori, back in October of

2018, had asked me to be the keynote speaker for a Women In Business Conference to be held at the Jacksonville Jaguars Stadium on May 18, 2013, only five days after I had been fired. Talk about God's timing! I barely had an opportunity to grieve my losses before a new opportunity had presented itself. In hindsight, I realize it was "the" opportunity that would set my life back on course for the new normal God had actually intended me to heal and grow within. I had just taken an unnecessary detour and gotten about as lost as a soul could get without GPS (God's Perfect System).

The speaking engagement didn't pay a lot in dollars and cents, but it was priceless because it offered me hope. What I felt and what I saw of my life prior to that day, was pain, frustration, failure, shame, confusion, worry, and doubt. I had no job AGAIN! For the first time ever in my life, I had been fired and I had to file for unemployment. I had to deal with the embarrassment of people constantly asking me why I wasn't with the university anymore. What happened? I had to ask my loyal seasonal employer, the Big Ten Network, if I could get my coveted analyst position back after having missed a season. Drew was more depressed than ever as I would have to uproot him again.

Drew had recently turned 15 years of age. In his lifetime, we had moved 13 times! This move back to Jacksonville would be the 4th since his brain surgery 3 years earlier. Drew grew to resent me for the lack of stability. I grew to resent myself too. Being fired after making yet another move in the midst of Drew's trauma was the self-inflicted insult to injury neither of us should have ever endured. That should have been enough consequence of a bad choice to teach me the lesson I needed to learn. And yet, there was another huge stabbing wound I'd have to endure from making decisions from a place of fear or vulnerability...

I had always been very independent and self-sufficient, even as a young child. As a single mom, I had accepted and embraced, more than I ever wanted to, the need to fulfill both the maternal and paternal roles in my son's life. Having that awesome, provider husband my mother always nagged me about, seemed like a fairy tale that would not happen for me anytime soon, so I became even more independent. But after surgery and the realization that rehabilitating a young child after a brain tumor, was the most uncertain, most unstable, scariest, and loneliest feeling I had ever experienced in 47 years of life, I suddenly believed I needed a man. I needed my helpmate. I needed strength, courage, protection, provision, companionship, and guidance. I truly both wanted and needed a man, someone, anyone, willing to love me and my son. I settled for Devilin Terry.

I did not actually know I was settling. In the beginning, love is blind, free, exciting, and new! I fell for Devilin quickly, in the midst of a million red flags I could not see. The ones I could see, I brushed aside, justified, or downright lied to myself that they did not exist. I was in love for the first time in almost 20 years. I had something to focus on other than the flagrant fouls I had been going through with Drew and Coach Killjoy. I met Devilin on an online dating site. It was shortly after he had survived a stroke and aneurism. He had lost his peripheral vision and strength in his arm on his left side. Mutual empathy for having endured flagrant fouls connected us instantly. But the red flags were there, red flags only hindsight and deep introspection after a couple of years of unnecessary pain, did I finally acknowledge. Even after I acknowledged them, a habit of strange normalcy from living in codependency and pain, still kept me from making the wise choice to permanently leave the relationship when I should have.

While this part of my life could easily become a bestselling novel, it was the one part of this book I wanted to share to illustrate the profound perspective that *what you currently see is not the same as what is meant to be.* People use the terms "sight" and "vision" interchangeably. They are not the same, to me. Sight is physical. It's tangible. It is the here and now. Given the adage of, "Seeing is believing," we trust what we see. Vision, however, is spiritual. It is intangible. It is the uncertain future, so we don't always trust it. That trust is called FAITH! Regardless of what you believe religiously, every one of us experiences vision, even if only little tiny glimpses, every day. Vision is that something that is placed inside of your spirit that allows you to dream and imagine. It is that something that says, "Do this thing you have never done before. Try this. Try that." It is that special, supernatural thing that encourages you to be your greatest self, and it invites you to trust it, even though you cannot actually see it.

Growth comes from trusting your vision, not trusting your sight. With Devilin, I was stuck in a terrible, vulnerable pattern of only trusting what I could see. This caused my vision to become clouded, warped, confused, and delayed. When it came to my relationship, I was far blinder than my son would ever be. Loneliness, sadness, depression, anxiety, and uncertainty: These were the things that were in my sight. Sure, I had hope that they would all greatly improve, but I lacked faith that there was already a plan in place for my life and for Drew's life far beyond what I could currently see. I became deeply entrenched with my co-dependent partner, whose dysfunctional version of love blinded me to what true vision and true love was all about.

Devilin had one remarkably, extraordinary gift. When things got rough and I did not think our relationship would work out, he was gifted at telling me exactly what I wanted and needed to hear. He could fall down on his knees and beg better than the Godfather of Soul himself! All he needed was a band, a cape, and a bad perm, and I'd swear I had my own personal James Brown! With tears and sobbing, he could present himself in such dire pain and agony that he swore only my love could fix. He would convince me that leaving him was his kryptonite, while believing in him would make him Superman.

Devilin could pull on my heartstrings of sympathy and guilt with the might of Hercules. He was always the victim, and aiming to manipulate, he thrived on my being such a social empath, a giver, and a fixer, which should have been a huge red flag for me. Every story was carefully plotted to get me to feel sorry for him. Deep down, my soul was screaming "get far away from this guy," but I'd acquiesce and question my compassion every time. Hadn't he suffered enough growing up poor, and neglected, having to fight for everything? Hadn't his father been horribly abusive? Hadn't his mother recently passed away? Hadn't he suffered enough almost losing his life? Hadn't he become disabled? Hadn't his ex-wife already treated him so poorly? She didn't even show up to see him in the hospital where he lay for one month! I remember thinking what a terrible person this woman must have been to be so cold to her own dying husband. Later, I deduced she wasn't cold at all - she was smart! She, too, was probably just fed up with trusting her sight instead of her vision.

By no means was Devilin a bad guy. Like everyone else, he had his ghosts and demons. Our good times together were great. But I fell for him for the wrong reasons. My family and friends say I have a huge heart and feel for others so very deeply. I fell in love because I am a giver, which unfortunately means I also have a bad habit of falling for takers, and for enabling people. I fell in love because I was lonesome and needy. I was dependent on "a" man, not "the" man God designed for me. I took my eyes off of God, the only true provider I needed, especially while playing through a flagrant foul. Only a person in pain, blinded by their own sight, would allow themselves to not trust their vision for a better future and make decisions accordingly.

Settling When Sight Hurts

The woman with a vision for her life would never find true or deep attraction to a man who did not work, had no reasonable plans to work, and overexaggerated and even faked some ailments so that he could receive a disability paycheck. But a woman whose sight said, "Well, at least, you have a man around, someone to help take the trash out from time to time and hold you at night when you feel sad and lonely," will and did continue to co-exist in a dysfunctional relationship. When that same woman has a man professing his love by begging for her to stay, insisting he would get a job and even volunteer at the church until he did, it sounds more attractive than you think. When that same woman is vulnerable, it is easy to buy into the false hope, or the manipulative vision, of the man she fiercely believes she loves.

Just as I was gaining the vision for my professional life, and it began to take off, my personal life really began to suffer. Devilin began showing tremendous signs of insecurity. I never even paid attention, at first, to how I began to constantly walk on eggshells around him. Slowly, I began to see how I constantly felt I was in defense of everything. The back and forth was just something I had never experienced before. Only once before had I entertained the interrogations of an insecure and jealous guy I dated. I dropped him like a snake mistaken for a garden hose! I never put up with that insecure, destructive behavior when I was strong and independent. But I had become only a shell of that woman, especially after my fiasco working for Coach Killjoy. I was broken more than I realized, and Devilin took full advantage.

It started out with repetitive, tiny inquiries: "Who were you talking to on the phone?" "Who's texting you?" "Why didn't you call me back right away?" "Why didn't you answer my text?" The next thing I knew, I was trying to defend things I didn't even know how to defend, because I couldn't believe I was being interrogated about things so ridiculous. It was my daily occurrence to get blindsided with Devilin's angry insinuations, accusations, and attacks. One day, he would be asking me about some guy who held the door open for me a week ago at a store I could barely remember even going into, let alone the guy. The next day, I was cheering too hard for the football player on TV.

The attacks became more personal and closer and closer to home. Once, a young, 23-year-old young man and his girlfriend moved in next door. We had never met. Devilin and I would always go out for morning walks together. Upon finishing up our walk one day, the young man was outside getting ready to wash his car. He greeted both of us, but Devilin, never one for social niceties, remained silent after the initial hello. I engaged the young man in a very brief, cordial conversation demonstrating nothing more than common courtesy and neighborly respect. When I came inside, I was blindsided with an attack from the big, angry bear!

"Why did you stay outside talking to him when you know you had shorts on? I saw him looking at you! He's a man! I know how men think! Don't try to act like you don't know he was looking at you!"

I remember chuckling because I looked a hot, smelly, sweaty mess! "Devilin, what could a 23-year-old, young enough to be my son, possibly want with this bad hair, gargoyle-looking, sweatbox? I just spent an hour walking through the neighborhood with you in these same workout clothes. When did they suddenly become so inappropriate? You're being ridiculous!" I defended sarcastically. It wasn't funny to Devilin. He maintained that I was being intentionally disrespectful. Per usual, the argument ensued. Two hours later, he'd be in apology mode, trying to wash the dishes or rub my feet or anything else he could think of to deflect my attention from his insecure behavior.

For months and months on end, the insecurities grew more prevalent and the attacks were no longer just about strangers, but people he knew and should have been very comfortable with. The closer people were to me, the harsher the attacks:

"Why are you still friends with your ex-husband? You know he still wants you back!" (Argument.)

"Your best friend doesn't like me. You know the only reason she asks you to go out with her is to hook you up with another guy, right? (Argument.)

"I don't like your gay friends. They just want you to be gay." (Argument.)

"I know your cousins don't like me. I don't like them either." (Argument.)

"Why does your dog always have to come around? Why do you always pet him? (Argument.)

"Why do you have so many friends? You trust too many people." (Argument.)

"I know Drew really doesn't like me. His father probably said something about me." (Argument.)

My life had just become one argument after another. I actually started believing arguing with your boyfriend and going out of your way to prove your love to calm his insecurities, possessiveness, and anger was just part of my new normal. I thought breaking up with him after a few months of putting up with the craziness and then having him fall on his knees to beg me to stay was normal. I thought him apologizing until the cows came home and making promises to be sweeter, less possessive, more romantic, get a good job, join the church, and go get the counseling I begged him to consider, was all normal. Every time, he'd swear I was the one he prayed for and he was one day going to marry me! I'd forgive. We'd have a great few days, then be right back at the same stuff the following week. It was one big cycle of codependent cuckoo for Cocoa Puffs!.

In my best psychological assessment, Devilin was a man, whom after recently almost losing his life to a stroke and aneurism, losing his wife to divorce, losing his job due to disability, losing his financial stability, losing his mother to cancer, losing his place to live, and begging to move in with me, had more fouls to play through than I did. It was complicated by the fact that he grew up in a very abusive home and had experienced tremendous poverty and neglect. Those old wounds were never mended and surfaced in the form of extreme social anxieties, insecurities, and anger. He was a sweet man, but his issues ran uncontrollably deep. With everything else I was going through, I knew this was not an ideal match. Yet I felt stuck and settled for what I saw, neglecting the vision that daily whispered, "Get out of the way. A better life is in store."

I needed to love him because he needed me to love him. I wanted to believe in him. I wanted him to win, and I thought as soon as he recognized my uncompromised commitment to him, we would win together. However, Devilin became more mentally unstable and it began to show itself in so many ways. The anger and insecurity became more and more unbearable. I had never seen anything like it outside of a movie or Law & Order SVU reruns. I began to start researching everything I could on bipolar behavior. He would become so angry, after a while it became contagious. I became irritable and anxious too. I wasn't positively affecting Devilin at all the way I had hoped. He instead was negatively affecting me.

My friends began to worry about me. Drew was always more distant when Devilin was around. I became far more stressed than I realized. I became so unconsciously stressed, that in June of 2014, while out walking/jogging with Devilin, I felt burning, hot, cramping pain in my chest and shooting down my left arm. It was hard to breathe. I had just delivered a keynote for the American Heart Association a month earlier. I had learned all the heart attack signs. I knew something was terribly wrong. Devilin had to jog back to the house, about a mile away, get the car, and come back to get me as I sat waiting outside under a shade tree at the gas station trying to calm down and praying this wasn't what I thought it was. It couldn't be!

Failing Heart

Fast forward, Devilin got me to the ER where I was immediately hospitalized for what the doctors believed was indeed a heart attack. For four days, I lay there, test after test, specialist after specialist, nurse after nurse, analyzing my life. I missed my first speaking engagement ever.

"How could this be? Mom died from a heart attack, so I know I'm a high-risk candidate. But she was 75, obese, and a former smoker. I'm only 48, a little overweight, but strong, athletic, and healthy," I reasoned.

I spent countless hours praying. A few very divine thoughts came into my spirit. I began to see the vision very clearly. I began to understand that the longer I held onto Devilin, the more my wellness, mind, body, and spirit would suffer. I had to get Devilin out of my sight if I were ever going to have a chance at achieving God's vision. I cried and I asked for courage. I was afraid to totally let go but I knew I had to.

When you love someone – I mean deep down, soul stirring, "play that love song again and again" love someone – getting them out of your sight, let alone your heart, is very hard to do. When the cardiologist revealed to me that I had stress-induced tachycardia, not a heart attack, I knew some things had to change. I still had an awesome, now 16-year-old son to raise. Trusting my vision was about him. He needed a blessed mom, not a stressed mom. As soon as I was stronger, I swore I would leave Devilin. True to form, right on cue, Devilin began to be on his best behavior again, so I began trusting my sight and not my vision again.

I would like to make a very important testimonial here because I know someone really needs to hear this. I understand and I empathize if you are *dangerously* in love with someone. I know what it is like to want to believe and stick out a troubled relationship in hopes that things will just get better. Honestly, no one empathizes with this better than me; but, please hear me out. When you won't adhere to the many red flags fiercely trying to wave you down (and a heart attack scare is about as fierce as they come), you are headed for a critical collision, and all the love and hope in the world for that someone won't save you.

In April of 2015, I was hospitalized again, but this time due to plan, not unexpected emergency. I had to have a hysterectomy, and it would require me to be on bed rest for a minimum of two weeks, then another four weeks before I could return to regular activities. Midway through recovery, I was also planning to sell my condo and move into a beautiful new home under construction. Devilin's anger issues were still prevalent, but I had changed a lot. I was no longer interested in stressing myself out in an argument just to feel like I had defended that which never needed defending. Devilin had definitely taken notice. When he would start in with the nitpicking, I would just get silent or go take a long walk to avoid it all. I would tell myself, "This isn't a brain tumor and it's not worth a heart attack, so it doesn't deserve my stress."

My professional life was taking off and Devlin occasionally joked that I might blow up into stardom so much that I probably would decide I didn't need a man like him anymore. He would say he didn't deserve someone like me. As the saying goes, "Many an honest word is spoken in jest." I was beginning to trust my vision and take steps to make a better living for Drew and me, but where Devilin would fit into that was a very big question mark. In the midst of my success, he was becoming more insecure and angry, and I pleaded with him to get some anger management counseling.

We had been together for well over two years. Devilin was well-healed from his stroke. He'd run six miles a day, but he had no interest in working. His disability check barely got him by, especially now that I insisted he lived in his own place. To appease me, he would start the conversations about getting a job somewhere but going out to the track to gamble or play the Lotto was as close as he would come. Meanwhile, although Devilin supported me on the surface, deep down, I knew he resented me for my growth.

I was no longer his depressed, emotionally needy, unemployed victim, or the caregiver who was traumatized and vulnerable. I was determined to become what Mom had told me to become, and then some! I had become a four-book author, a motivational speaker, a corporate trainer, a women's basketball analyst, all at one time, and now about to make a good profit on the condo foreclosure I had invested in four years earlier. I was finally financially stable, and I needed a man who shared my work ethic and commitment to build together. After everything we had been through together, I still wanted Devilin to be that man (I told you love is blind!), but I began to just accept he was not part of my vision.

On a fateful day in May, Cinco de Mayo to be exact, Devilin was in one of those moods to nitpick and argue. I just had no energy left, and no desire for senseless drama that would only move us backwards. I had begun packing up things in the days prior to my surgery, so there were a few boxes in my living room. Slowly and gingerly, I had made my way downstairs in an effort to just avoid another argument. Devilin stood about six feet, seven inches tall. I am 5 feet, eight inches tall, but I stood a couple of inches shorter on this day as I was still healing, and it was important to keep pressure on my midsection. So I had mastered the art of the, small gait, little old lady walk, hunched over as if I had scoliosis.

I was sitting on the sofa when Devilin made a comment I said I did not totally agree with. The next thing I knew, he had crouched down to put his face directly into mine and began shouting at me that I thought I knew everything. This was a common theme, a show I had seen many times, so I decided this was the very last episode I ever wanted to watch. This time, Devilin was too close and too angry over nothing, and it really scared me a little. I turned my face away from his and I immediately eyed his large 29-inch rolling suitcase in the living room, next to the kitchen counter. He had packed it to take his clothes back to his apartment. Without saying a word, slowly, I rose up off the couch, clasping my mid-section as I did the hunchback walk over to his bag.

"Where the (expletive) do you think you're going, Vera?" he shouted, with his nostrils flared and spit flying from his mouth.

I placed my hand on the handle of his suitcase. I inhaled deeply, then dropped my head and shoulders in complete disengagement. I shook my head, and I took my time. "Devilin, I'm done. I just want you to take your suitcase and leave. Go home. I'm done arguing. This just isn't working anymore. It hasn't been working for a long time. It's over. Please just go."

Before I could blink, Devlin had leaped across the living room in a single bound! In what felt like one continuous motion of rage, he snatched the suitcase handle out my hand and screamed, "You're always trying to leave me and I'm sick of it!" Then he used both hands to shove me backwards. I flipped over a box behind me and came crashing into another couple of boxes stacked behind it. It happened so fast! Suddenly, I was on the ground clasping my incision, instantly praying I had not started bleeding internally. With my eyes popping out of my head in disbelief and tears popping out of my eyes in pain, I looked up and saw Devilin coming towards me. I thought he had realized what he had done and was coming to see if I was okay or help me up. Instead, he stood over me and began to scream even more! His eyes were peering through me, like he didn't even know who I was!

No matter how many times we had ever argued before, in a million years, I would have told anyone who asked that Devilin was harmless, more bark than bite. Holy Smokes, he just bit! He kept biting! "I hate you, Vera! I hate you! You're always trying to leave somebody! You think you're better than me? Well (expletive) you! (Expletive) you, then! I hope you rot in (expletive!) I don't need your ass anyway! There are plenty of women out here that want me!"

I was crying hysterically, "Get away from me, Devilin!" I felt the tachycardia kick in as I lay there helpless. It hurt to move, and I was so afraid of the internal damage that had just been done. More than anything, I was in shock. Did this big, skinny, growling bear really put his hands on me? No man had ever put his hands on me! And he looked like he was ready to do even more damage. His eyes were so menacing. I had never seen them like that before. Not once did he even look like he wanted to help me up. He seemed to revel in my tears, in my pain, and seeing me in a place where he could finally make me sure I was lower than him. Towering over me, he screamed one last, "You ain't (expletive). I'm gladly leaving!"

At this point, I began crawling as swiftly as I could to the staircase. I had left my cellphone upstairs. I started repeating my thoughts aloud, "I've got to call 911. I've got to call 911." I held my incision as I managed to sit on the first stair, then crouching over, I raised my butt to the next stair, and then the next. Devilin overheard me saying I was going to call 911 and just as he got to the front door came rushing back in yelling, "You calling the police on me, Vera? You better not call the police!"

It hurt too much to yell. While crying, I just kept saying, "Get away from me, Devilin. Please get away from me!" Devilin stormed off again, slamming the front door. I made it to the top of the stairs and crawled down the hall to my bedroom. I immediately grabbed my phone and called 911! Just when I thought he was gone, Devilin came bursting through the bedroom door. Yes, like the dumb girl in the horror movies, I forgot to lock the door. Don't judge me, I was too much in shock. He began listening to my conversation screaming, "I can't believe you are calling the police on me! Hang up the phone, Vera!"

"Is he there with you, ma'am? Can you get to a place of safety? Stay on the phone with me. A car has been dispatched and is on the way! Hang in there with me. What is he doing now?" The female dispatcher was trying to assure my safety and location.

The rest of the story was a complete nightmare in the daytime. There were so many more twists and turns to this madness, it truly does deserve its own book. It was a tale of a lot of emotional, degrading firsts for me. I had to file a restraining order. I had to contact a domestic abuse center. I had to deal with fear and nightmares that he may be stalking me, waiting for his opportunity to return. I blocked his phone and avoided going anywhere I thought he may be. How could we have gotten to this point? How could love turn to such damage and destruction? I was embarrassed to see my neighbors, and to even tell my closest friends. I was most embarrassed to have to tell Drew and my dad.

Why did learning the lesson of sight vs. vision have to hurt so much? Why was love so very blind? Why wasn't I obedient to the holy spirit voice long ago that told me to leave? Who had I become and when would I ever look in the mirror again and actually like what I see? When would my purpose and dignity ever stare back? So many questions and nothing but pain and sorrow for answers.

Hurting, Healing, Seeing

Some things will never truly permeate our minds, hearts, and spirits unless they cause us pain. My pain was not just emotional, but also it left a very physical reminder. The infamous shoving incident led to a ruptured disc and sciatic nerve pain that required yet another surgery only four months post-hysterectomy recovery. I struggle with lower back issues and nerve pain to this day. It took a very debilitating event to teach me a lesson I will never forget. It is a lesson I had to find great courage to finally open up about and share. I was so embarrassed to become a domestic violence statistic. I didn't want anyone to know that I, an accomplished broadcaster, a motivational speaker, and leadership coach, had this much dysfunction in my own personal life. Who would I be then to be giving anyone any advice, when I couldn't even get my own life together?

Great question! I had finally become just who I needed to be. I became wiser in my misguided belief that I could fix everything and everybody myself. And I was humbled to more deeply, and more empathically understand a lot more about relational fouls than I had ever known before. I certainly did it the hard way, but maybe my lesson can be someone else's blessing. I truly believe there is a low point that inevitably forces a person to fully let go in complete surrender to the reverence and grace of God. In this space, He can use you for His purpose because you recognize you are no longer in control and have no choice but to just get out of the way.

I cried out, "Enough already! It's yours! All of the hurt; the pain; the anger; the shame; the firing; the unemployment; the desire for revenge; the relationship drama; the domestic abuse; the brain tumor; the blindness; the self-sabotage; the sciatica; the surgeries; the depression; Drew's depression; Drew's suicidal thoughts; being broke; being broken; mom's death...JESUS, TAKE IT AWAY! How much more of this can one woman possibly take, make, or break? TAKE EVERY BIT OF IT AWAY!"

I wanted and needed total, divine healing. No more scab picking. No more trusting just my sight when God was trying to teach me to trust His vision for my life. It was a vision that could not possibly have been any clearer. Mom told me exactly what to do with my life here on earth, and then she passed on into eternal life. Until I learned to trust that vision completely, with no peripheral distractions; until I learned to stay focused and move ahead one step at a time toward that goal; until I learned to ask for help when I needed it; until I found the courage to be obedient to the things I needed to do because I could; until I learned to trust in my new normal instead of forcing one; I would inevitably be unnecessary pain. I would not grow to understand that what you currently see can become blinding, and you will miss who it is you are meant to be. The minute I grasped all of that was the minute I knew I was healed.

Long gone are the days of being bitter, because vision has finally made me better. I actually thank Coach Killjoy. I thank Devilin Terry. Albeit uncomfortable, we were all necessary to each other's journeys. They, too, were just lost and hurting human beings trying to find their way with, from what I can tell, far less vision than I had. My blessings began to overflow the moment I just let go. The fouls that seemed to just happen, we began to humbly accept as part of the game. The people we believed caused them, did not blind Drew and me more, because we learned to open up the eyes of our souls to forgiveness. I also learned to forgive myself, and breathed freedom in doing so. Fouls, even flagrant ones, are necessary obstacles for us to have greater appreciation for life, hope, faith, and God!

When people would come up to me and say, "I'm so sorry that Drew lost his vision," I would gently correct them to say he actually didn't lose his vision, he lost his sight. I didn't mean to be petty or play on semantics, but I had learned the difference, and I had learned that words are so very powerful. Just like my mother spoke into my life, I had spoken, and will continue to speak into my son's. I am absolutely confident the vision for his life is far greater than his sight. I had gained very personal and intrinsic wisdom in this. We've played through some pretty rough, flagrant fouls together, and after I let go of the things sight told me I needed, and opened up to what vision had already prepared, an entirely new life opened up for both of us. There was now one lesson we both graciously learned. On to my final and favorite lesson to share.

REFLECTION: Sight is physical. We trust it because it is the here, the now, the tangible. Vision is spiritual. It is that something special, deep inside of you, challenging you to move towards a divine purpose. Will you trust it even if you cannot physically see it? What is it you've been wanting to do for so long? What is that voice you've been sensing telling you to step out on faith and make something awesome happen?

Vision invites you every day to be better, stronger, wiser, happier, more at peace, etc., and to move towards your Creator. Sometimes, Vision will even go beyond a thought or feeling and boldly introduce itself in the form of prophetic words. Sight often becomes blinding and painful because it's time to act on Vision. Remember, Sight is perception of your present. Vision is faith in your future! It's not about what you can see. It's about who you are meant to be! If you want to grow into your purpose, Trust Your Vision!

CHAPTER 11

SIGNIFICANCE AND PURPOSE

THIS JOURNEY BEGAN in 2007, 12 years ago from the writing of this book. It was the year my mother died suddenly from a heart attack in the midst of March Madness. Feeling expectedly melancholy one day, in April of that year, I just didn't have the energy to go into a big supermarket full of people. I opted to try out a small corner grocery just outside the Indiana University college campus. I remember pulling into the store with my friend John and Drew. We were just going to quickly pop in, pick up a few items, then return to the house where we were packing up for my upcoming move.

I was at the counter about to check out. Drew had convinced John to come help him play "The Claw" at the entrance of the store. Drew had developed a voracious obsession with the big, square, glass tower of toys and candy some wily human being designed just to rip off little boys and girls who couldn't resist begging for quarters from their parents. Meanwhile, I was delivering my money into the hands of the cashier who pleasantly thanked me for my purchase and was about to hand me my receipt.

I GOT IT!

Unexpectedly, I was startled by a young man whom I first captured in my right peripheral. He obnoxiously and abruptly was sprinting towards me! I turned my head quickly, and as I took him in full gaze, he began screaming at the top of his lungs, "I GOT IT!" The man was screaming like someone calling for help in a horror movie! Now I admit, I am one of those creative right brain types, prone to occasional storytelling embellishment, but I promise you I'm not taking that liberty now. "I GOT IT!" he shouted, loud enough to start a fire drill.

Drew spun around from playing "The Claw," John instinctually began to move in my direction for defensive protection, and it felt like every eye in the store was wide-eyed gazed upon the mad, dashing, screaming man running towards me! I felt a wave of heat rush through my chest and a tightening of my jaw as my eyes widened in fear and disbelief. Once he approached me, he came to a clumsy halt and, with his left forearm against my right, pushed me away from my cart! Like most women, my purse was in the small basket area by the handlebar.

I'm not sure where you are from, but I grew up in Prince George's County, MD outside our nation's capital. Where I'm from, when some stranger comes running towards you, screaming like a madman, and pushes you away from your own pocketbook in your shopping cart, it's time to get ready for your big chance to be featured on the nightly news! Eyebrows furrowed, jaw tight, heart racing, fists clinched, and an arsenal of curse words lined up and ready for oral- missile launch, my fight or flight said, "Fight!" I deemed my Christian values and goodwill towards all men were forgivably null and void at this moment!

Face to face we stood, and again, the scream, "I GOT IT!" bellowed from deep inside this strange man's throat! Instead of screaming back at him or doing my best Karate Kid impression, I stood in frozen silence, as this time his exclamation was followed by his slurred speech. It sounded like, "Riiicc-kkeee-poosh-da-carts!" I squinted and stared deeply into his face, and although instinctively, I was certain I was going to ball up my fist and punch him as hard as I could, my heart instead was softened and humbled beyond anything I had ever experienced.

At that very moment, I stared into this young man's face and I noticed that not only did he slur his speech, but also he had a bit of a facial deformity as well. His eyes were droopy, but soft behind his thick-framed glasses. His mouth slightly hung open, suggesting a smile that hadn't quite figured out how to form, but had a lot of pure potential. Thankfully, I was wise enough to understand, even in duress, that he likely had a learning disability or intellectual challenge of some sort. The light bulb clicked on. This peculiar young man wasn't trying to steal my purse or cause me bodily harm in broad daylight in front of a host of startled and bewildered onlookers. He was trying to *help* me! He was passionately, proudly, and powerfully taking ownership of the job he had been asked to do. He was saying in the best way he knew how, "No, Lady, in this store, it is my duty and my honor to push the carts. I cannot allow you to do it for this is *my job, my gift, my pleasure, my passion, and it is my purpose!*"

"I GOT IT!" Three very simple but powerful words. "Ricky, push the carts!" Confession. I've been telling this story for over a decade and the truth is that I really don't know what this young man's name really was. His speech was slurred, and this was the best interpretation I could come up with in such an awkward and tense moment. But his name has lived on in legacy now as "Ricky" to me and everyone I tell this story to. "Ricky, push the carts!" And that he did! He swung my cart into the aisle (with my purse still in it!) and off he went, full steam ahead, out of the store. Drew and John were both cutting their eyes at me to make sure I was okay while simultaneously trying not to laugh. I just followed my purse out the store, making sure to stay completely out of Ricky's way! "Let the man do his job," I always say!

We reached the car and I popped open the trunk. I placed a few bags in the trunk, checking first with Ricky to be sure it was all right for me to do so, of course. I didn't want to find out the hard or painful way that "Ricky packs the trunk, too!" When the cart was empty, Ricky looked at me again and said, "I GOT IT!" to reassure me it was his pleasure serving me. Off he went pushing the cart back towards the grocery store. When he entered the store, in the distance, we saw him running towards the checkout line and then heard him scream "I GOT IT!" startling the daylights out of the next unsuspecting customer!

"Go, Ricky!" I instantly became his number one fan!

Unsuspected Inspiration

For the remaining weeks I was in Bloomington, Indiana, I could not get "I GOT IT" out of my head. I'd see Ricky's face, and I would pause whatever I was doing to just smile and admire his tenacity of purpose. In those moments where I was down, or when I woke up less than optimistic, I would stare into the mirror, yell "I GOT IT!" and smile. It was hard not to smile every time I thought of him. I even went back to shop at that grocery a few times just to see if he was there. It was easy to know when he was. I could hear "I GOT IT!" off in the distance when I was parking my car. I couldn't wait to see the reactions of the various customers. Ricky inspired me. Ricky made me feel good about being alive, even as I grieved my mother who no longer was.

Unbeknown to him, Ricky regularly made me laugh, too. When we were being silly around the house, Drew and I would scream "I GOT IT!" just to catch each other off-guard. When John would come over to visit, he'd ring the doorbell and I'd scream, "I GOT IT! Vera, open the door!" John would scream "I GOT IT!" right back. Later Drew, holding the remote would scream, "I GOT IT! Andrew, change the channels!" "I GOT IT! Mom, wash the dishes!"

This silliness went on in my household for the longest time and it always brought a smile to my face. Smiling was something I was in dire need of at the time. Lightheartedness and laughter are great medicine for the ailing soul. Yet there was something so much more, well, *significant*, about Ricky's story. It was such a bizarre incident that didn't just help me to smile and go through a tough time, but also it helped me illustrate to myself and others how to *grow* through a tough time.

When you are going through the fouls of life, it is easy to take your mind off of the goal. Many of us go through life, not knowing the goal at all. I could not wait to write this chapter, saving the best for last, because I may not know much, but the basketball player in me knows a whole lot about scoring the goal! The opponent, the enemy, the negative forces of the universe or the spiritual realm, do not want you to score. The best way for this to happen is to foul you hard enough when you are in the game to take you out of it. The enemy wins if you never get back in, because then you do not do the very things God, our ultimate coach, put you here to do. The flagrant fouls of life are capable of causing that kind of injury, unless you understand and passionately embrace this most essential lesson: YOU ARE SIGNIFICANT!

In that very moment, on that very day, in that grocery store parking lot, I could feel in my spirit, my encounter with Ricky was meant to be more than just another story to tell about an amusing or confusing moment. My encounter with Ricky was to help me understand the power of significance. The goal of life and leadership is to be significant. It is not to be important, it is not to be successful, it is not to be rich, although you couldn't tell that from the media, politics, or the state of our prevailing societal agendas and culture. We live in an "it's all about me" world. I've often lectured that, yes, it actually is all about you, for a little while. It should be so that you can learn who you are and whose you are. But I guarantee, once you learn that, you will find, "It's only about you long enough for you to discover it was really never about you, at all. It was, it is, and it will always be about serving others!"

Cheat Sheet: Why We Are Here

Significance is achieved through service and service is the reason why you are here. There you have it. For everybody searching for purpose, I just gave you the cheat sheet! We are all here to serve God, and we obediently and best accomplish this by serving others. Each of us has been given a gift, or gifts, of purpose. Your opposition, or enemy, never wants you to know what those gifts are, let alone how to use them and for whom to use them. I'm telling you the way to score and win, and to keep on winning, is to keep on serving. To do this, you have to be willing to play through your fouls. You have to be willing to embrace just how significant you truly are. There is nothing worse than living a life feeling like you don't matter. The enemy knows this well and will continue to use this to his advantage.

When you experience life's hardest fouls, when you feel vulnerable, unworthy, lost, sad, empty, depressed, and defeated, how can you possibly be significant in helping someone else realize their significance? If no one ever feels significant; no one desires to be of service; everyone just looks out for themselves or gives into feelings of defeat and insignificance. We, of course, then perish as a people. I'm not implying that we should never take time for ourselves, to breathe, to analyze, or to heal. I am saying that when you have a sense of purpose, a sense of how you matter and why you matter, your desire to heal has a greater sense of necessity and urgency.

Ricky epitomized this and gave me a major aha moment, as well as a platform speech and leadership training lesson for the future. Here was a young man, who with a learning disability, probably had faced more fouls in his young life than I would ever experience in all of mine. Yet, in my entire life, I had not met anyone more passionate, more focused, more committed, to his job of serving others so enthusiastically than Ricky. To so many, I'm sure pushing grocery carts seemed like a menial task. To Ricky, it was his chance to show, "I can!" It was his chance to show, "I serve with a purpose." It was his chance to show, "I am significant, and I want to help you because you are significant, too!"

It did not matter to Ricky if others noticed he was awkward or loud. It didn't matter if he was looked upon with ridicule or pity because he had been fouled with a disability. It didn't matter if they laughed or ignored him with indifference. When it was time to push the carts, Ricky had no peripheral distractions. He moved towards his goal one cart and customer at a time, and he passionately played his position! I literally well up with emotion every time I stand on stage and tell his story. It is my personal favorite example of why we are all here, and why we have to passionately play our positions in life, in spite of the fouls. We matter, and we always have the purpose of serving others and making a difference for good, even if we are simply pushing their carts. Having the mindset of significance, kick-starts the healing process necessary to help us play through any foul we face.

My son was always my priority. He was an obvious outlet for my significance. No matter what I was feeling on any given day, including the ones I just wanted to give up, there was always the subconscious tugging on my spirit that I was needed. Drew needed his mother to help guide, nurture, and comfort him through a most traumatic and flagrant time. It was in knowing this that I constantly strived to just get past my own pain to be there for him. Most parents feel this, naturally. Even when we go deep into our own pity parties of life, an opportunity to be significant, to help one of our children, reminds us of why we are here. But you don't have to be a parent; you just have to be aware and care just a little about others. There is always an opportunity to be significant, at work, at a children's hospital, at an elderly center, at church, for your neighbor, and definitely at the grocery store. For every foul that is holding you down one day, there are countless opportunities to get back up and be significant the next.

Overcoming adversity in life requires the trust that you serve a purpose greater than your pain. In fact, it is your pain, your fouls of life, that serves as the biggest and best way to get your attention when you take your mind off the goal. We are all here, with our gifts, talents, flaws, and fouls, to lead and serve everybody else. You matter, and your ability to play through life's fouls, especially the flagrant ones, matters too. Ricky taught me that. It is understanding that I am significant, that there is purpose in my pain, that makes me shout "I GOT IT!" every day. My big hope is that in reading this book, you now got it, too!

Hindsight Gratitude

I think one of the greatest gifts God gives us is hindsight. I could not have even written this book adequately had it not been for the blessing of hindsight. In 2007, there was no way for me to know that my mother's words would prove prophetic. In the immediate pain of losing my mother, I wondered how I would even make it through the next day, let alone find the time and commitment required to write a book. Upon completion of this book, I would have written five! Even long after her passing, my mother's words live on in significance to my life. How amazing is that? Only in looking back do I get to marvel at that blessing.

In 2010, when the neurosurgeon told me that my son may not live, or he may be blind if he did; when he was being bullied in middle school for being blind and different, and he became depressed and withdrawn from even wanting to go to school; I had no way of knowing he'd graduate high school as a salutatorian and receive academic scholarships to Florida State University. Next year, Drew is due to walk across that FSU graduation stage and go off into the world with a degree in Interdisciplinary Social Sciences. He has a vision of helping people, ideally persons with disabilities. When he can, Drew joins me on the speaking circuit, taking time to participate in diversity and disability forums and youth leadership panels. He even performs standup comedy in his leisure time! Who knew? Hindsight allows us to look back now and see that his flagrant fouls weren't designed to break him, but to bend him into trusting his vision to find his significance and purpose.

In 2013, when I was fired from the university where I encountered many emotional and psychological challenges with Coach Killjoy, I did not, could not, know I was being groomed to become a better empathic leadership and communications trainer. My work grew from providing basic team-building sessions for a day into providing year-long conflict resolution strategies for various clients. Having a fresh and personal perspective of what an employee might be experiencing at work, like feeling a lack of significance and security, or ways that executive or managerial leadership may be negatively affecting performance, was the perfect foundation to help me help others overcome adversity by building trust in their relationships at work. Such a rewarding career that offered me so much significance was never in my sight. Thank God for the vision!

I also could not see how much a negative work experience would open my eyes to my true purpose. I could not see there was an emotionally, spiritually, as well as financially rewarding career awaiting me as an inspirational speaker and author. Every day, I'm finding it really isn't a career at all; it is my calling, a prophecy fulfilled. I'm pretty sure my mother is rolling her "I told you so" eyes in Heaven right now! Every single foul I had to play through was absolutely necessary for my maturity and growth.

Empathetic by nature, who better to help others dig deeper to experience how they can become more compassionate towards others? How could I possibly become a thought leader about overcoming adversity if I never really faced any? How could faith and fortitude become my platform to coach if I had never learned to rely on those essential virtues to play through the difficult fouls of my own life? Sight never granted me these wonders. Vision did. I arrived at significance and purpose the moment I learned to trust it.

In October of 2017, that trust led me to a viral video that garnered 43 million views on a single Goalcast Facebook thread, plus countless other YouTube channels. Every day, my inbox was flooded with people reaching out to say "thank you" or "you helped me today." They were sharing with me their struggles and stories of despair and hopelessness. To think just by sharing my story, I could make a difference in that many people's lives. It was humbling and overwhelmingly powerful. On days when my significance feels a little challenged, I go back and read some of those comments and I'm charged instantly to keep pressing forward. I wipe away my pity party tears, and I scream "I GOT IT" and keep it moving!

On the B.E.N.C.H.

These are my revelations and meaningful aha moments, but what about yours? What flagrant fouls have you experienced that may be blinding your hope and stealing the faith needed to activate your vision? *In the hard times, I've often found comfort in knowing the God I cannot fully understand or see, fully understands and sees me.* Vision comes from your Creator. He alone defines your purpose. In spite of what you or anyone else sees; in spite of what you or anyone else feels; your life has been designed with significance to provide a very specific servant purpose. I want to leave as I began, on a basketball note, if you will indulge me for a few moments more. I have shared this lesson countless times with my audiences and coaching clients, because it is so very important to remember.

Back where we started this journey together, in Bloomington, IN, when Andrew was about eight years old, and just beginning to take an interest in basketball, he came to me with a very important question. Overly analytical and inquisitive since birth, he began, "Mom, what's the hardest position to play in basketball?"

"The hardest position to play, Drew?"

"Yes, what is the hardest position to play? Like, is it the point guard, because he is the one who has to dribble the ball up the court and call the plays like the quarterback?"

"No, it's not the point guard," I responded, amused at his sudden interest.

"Oh, I know," he continued with determination for discovery, "it's the center, right, Mom? Because he is the big guy in the middle like Shaq, Shaquille O'Neal, who always gets fouled and has to get all the rebounds, right?"

"No, it's not the center either, sweetie," I answered thoughtfully.

Impatiently, he grilled me, "Then what's the hardest position to play?"

I took a deep breath and attempted to reason and educate my precocious son. "Drew, the hardest position to play in basketball is also the hardest position to play in life – it's the position when you aren't playing."

"Huh?" Drew curled his little lips up and tried to twist his brow in a way that always made me chuckle when he didn't understand me.

I laughed. "Sweetie, the hardest position to play is when you are on the bench! It's on the bench when you will face the greatest frustration in basketball, and in life, because you're not getting the chance to do what you really want to do."

"Oh," Drew answered.

I giggled as he walked away. His face was contorted like he just bit into a bad piece of fruit. However, let me sweeten that fruit a little. To make it a bit easier to digest, I want to share a final story of how I arrived at the lessons I share about being on the bench.

Growing up in Fort Washington, Maryland, coming out of Friendly High School, I thought I was quite the superstar. After all, they had put my name in the Washington Post and the USA Today. I was a hoops phenom with a bright future receiving a full scholarship to Syracuse University! Off I went with my fresh 1984, bad-hair Jheri curl with a shag in the back, thinking I was Ms. All Hoops World destined to become a collegiate All-American basketball star, or maybe the first woman in the NBA! I ran into one, small but major problem. You see, apparently, my coach did not read the Washington Post or the USA Today! She sat me on the bench!

All of my dreams and desires came crashing to a halt! Who was she to do this to me? If you were playing high school girls' basketball, in my day, and you were the star of the team, you were likely, legitimately the only star, or maybe one of two really good, collegiate level players. When you arrived at a Division 1, NCAA program, everybody was the star of their respective teams too. I had always gotten by on my talent and athleticism. Now a true, grinding, burning, daily work ethic was required. Shocker! What on earth was that? The learning curve was fierce and if you weren't ready, then you found yourself in a most unusual place, on the bench.

What I know about life's parallels to basketball is that there will be many times where you may find yourself on the bench, and sometimes you will be in pain and confusion as you sit there. If the pain is great enough, you may not see yourself getting off of it. Vision says differently!

Years ago, I developed an acronym to help you understand the reasons why you might be on the bench. Keep in mind, first of all, that your greatest opportunity to grow is not when you are playing the game, and everything is going your way. Your greatest opportunity to grow is in your being on the B.E.N.C.H. Given that understanding, the bench is not a negative thing; it is a necessary thing.

B = Breathe

Think of that basketball player that has been going so hard, nonstop, up and down the court. Let's take me in the 1980s at Syracuse University, for instance. Sweat is flying, I'm breathing loudly, rapidly, and heavily, and my wet, curly, Jheri curl perm looks like the result of mating a lamb with a wet cat! It's pretty ugly. Coach calls a time out, for no other reason but to have me to catch my breath (and maybe to stroke my hair back a few times so as not to frighten the children in the stands!) Sometimes, you go so fast in life, you will find that things stop going the way you want them, because you are not as efficient. You need to rest, relax, or regroup. Keep in mind, there's a second half to play. This bench moment is a chance to prepare you for a challenging second half, and you will need to be well-rested and focused to get the win. If you are injured, remember, that bench moment may be a long one. Don't rush it.

E = Evaluate

I hated being on the bench. I'd pout, complain, roll my eyes, suck my teeth, and make up new and improved names to call my coach under my breath. When none of that seemed to work, I was left to just think about why I was really there. Coach had mentioned something about my not playing defense, or not running the play. Could it be that I needed to listen and be more obedient and accountable? When you are on the bench, you are being allowed the time to truly evaluate and analyze the reason, or reasons, why you are not where you want to be, playing the game the way you love to play it. This bench moment time is the best time to become an analyst. I happen to attribute being able to be a basketball analyst for over 30 years to the lessons I learned on the bench of the game just as much, if not more, than what I learned from being on the floor actually playing. Take the time to learn why you're benched and how to change and get back in the game.

N = Nurture

Sitting on the bench my freshman year in college allowed me to nurture patience and new perspectives. When I finally realized none of my pouting antics were going to get me back in the game, I also began to learn patience. I learned some things are just out of my control. I was not the decision maker. I also learned to not beat myself up. I learned that *the goal was not to be approved but improved.* I never thought about being improved when I was out there playing the game because if I was out there playing, I must've been doing something right. The criticism I received from my coach was to help make me better. I thought it was that she just didn't like me. You will see the game from a whole new perspective on the bench that you could not see while you are playing. Nurture feelings of patience, hope, new ways to improve, and optimistic perspectives while you are on the bench, and watch how much you elevate your game when you get back in!

C = Cheer

I always loved the applause. It wasn't that I was conceited. It's that I loved knowing I was doing something right, that I was good at something. Sitting on that bench at Syracuse, I learned everybody else loved that feeling too, and that there were plenty of other teammates that were doing great things to help our team win. If I couldn't get off that bench, I became determined to do a great job of being the best cheerleader I could from it for others! I was so animated on the bench a photojournalism major chose me as his subject for a contest and won an award! It wasn't a photo gallery of the star player; it was a gallery of the star encourager from the bench!

Sometimes, it will stimulate your soul to new heights if you feel the significance of cheering for, and encouraging, others. It takes your mind off of what's not going right with you to be of assistance to something going well for someone else, or for the team overall. Sometimes, you are on the bench because you need to be reminded it's not all about you.

H = Hunger

This, to me, was the biggest lesson of all. It speaks volumes for the purpose in the pain. The "H" of the bench is about your hunger, or what I call the Resilience Test. While sitting on the bench as a freshman at Syracuse, I admit now, in hindsight, it was the best thing for me. But while I was going through it, I hated the feeling of wanting to contribute more and being told I wasn't ready, I wasn't good enough, I needed to learn more, etc. I wanted to play, bad! I was miserable.

When on the bench, I came to realize, one of two things will eventually happen. Once you get tired of being in a place of mediocrity or repetitive negativity, you will either just quit (as I threatened to do a hundred times in my mind) or you will dig down, deep within your spirit and find the hunger to do everything in your power to get better and live out your dream. There's where that work ethic thing came in. Desire, passion, grit, determination, focus, faith, and fortitude; it's all in the hunger! Your being on the bench of your life is inviting you to dig deep and decide just how bad you want to fulfill the vision God has for you. You always have a choice.

That's the beauty and the power of the B.E.N.C.H. I went from riding the bench at Syracuse University as a freshman, to becoming a Conference Scholar Athlete of the Year award winner and a Hall of Fame and Letter Winner of Distinction Inductee many years later. Even more importantly, I became part of two Big East Championship teams. I came to understand the adversity, the fouls – big and small, always existed to make me better, not bitter. I came to understand that the challenges in life were so much like the challenges in sport, designed to help us learn perseverance pays off.

The biggest and best lesson of all on my life's journey, was to come to the understanding that the flagrant fouls - like having your child born with a hearing impairment and being diagnosed with a brain tumor that would leave him visually impaired and medically challenged twelve years later – still had purpose. When in your sight, there is nothing but pain, that is the time you have to begin, more than ever before, to trust your vision. When you learn to trust your vision, and you pursue it with faith and fortitude, in spite of the fouls, you will arrive at a place of significance and purpose. It is the most awesome place in the universe to be!

I will never be blind to that again. I can honestly say, beyond the shadow of a doubt, NOW I SEE! Because I listened to my mother's prophecy, I fought through the pain, and I found my purpose, it is my hope that you too, in reading this, now see! Now if you will excuse me, I have to go call Oprah!

REFLECTION: There is nothing more fulfilling than finally know-ing why you are here. For every piece of pain, there is a powerful piece of purpose. Don't lose faith and don't lose the fortitude necessary to arrive there. God is always in empathic control and has designed you to achieve something specific and special. Your vision is tied to your purpose and your purpose is always tied to significance in service.

Do you sometimes feel saddened by how much affliction, confusion, anger, and hate exists in the world? No matter how difficult or lonely life feels; no matter how many mistakes you have made; and no matter how much pain you experience; we are all here for a reason, to serve some specific good. You must believe, beyond what you currently see, that you are here to serve a purpose so much greater than you can imagine. You matter. You are Significant. So, enjoy the journey and keep playing to win! God Bless You and Your Beautiful Purpose.

Vera

REFERENCES

1 Atherton, Laurel. *To My Daughter: a Few Words from the Heart.* Blue Mountain Arts, Inc., 2005.

2 Worsham, Vickie M. *Remember What Is Most Important...* Blue Mountain Arts, Inc., 2005.

3 "Craniopharyngioma." St. Jude's Children's Research Hospital. 2019, https://www. stjude.org/disease/craniopharyngioma.html

4 Verma, Prakhar. "Destroy Negativity from Your Mind with This Simple Exercise." Mission.org. 27 Nov. 2017, https://medium.com/the-mission/a-practical-hack-to-combat-negative-thoughts-in-2-minutes-or-less-cc3d1bddb3af